The Wild Life I've Led

THE WILD LIFE I'VE LED

Stuart Trueman

Illustrated by the Author

McClelland and Stewart

ISBN: 0-7710-8600-8

The Canadian Publishers
McClelland and Stewart Limited
25 Hollinger Road, Toronto M4B 3G2

Printed and bound in Canada

Contents

Books by Stuart Trueman

Cousin Elva, 1955.

The Ordeal Of John Gyles, 1966; *reissued in 1973 in paperback.*

You're Only As Old As You Act, 1969; *Stephen Leacock Award for Humour.*

An Intimate History Of New Brunswick, 1970; *reissued in 1972 in paperback.*

My Life As A Rose-Breasted Grosbeak, 1972.

The Fascinating World Of New Brunswick, 1973.

Ghosts, Pirates and Treasure Trove, 1975.

To my wife,
who for so many years
has cheerfully tolerated
all these wild creatures
and myself as well.

Introduction

If you love animals and birds, it's easy to forgive them for their occasional small transgressions – for the times they frustrate you, embarrass you, worry you to death and cost you a lot of money.

The point is, they don't mean it at all. I know that raccoons are regarded as the Dr. Jekyll and Mr. Hyde of the nature world – but they're not really vandals merely because they tear the stuffing out of mattresses and sofas. They aren't vindictive; they're just curious – they want to see what's inside.

I didn't fume when our pet raccoons squeezed through tiny crevices, got in the garage, broke into our younger son's camping equipment, scattered mustard all over the floor, and ate the dehydrated foods. Instead I fretted over the possibility that when they drank water and the foods began to swell up, we'd hear raccoons popping like punctured balloons all over the place. Nothing happened, which shows Mother Nature must be ahead of the rest of us – she's found a way to install an effective anti-inflation program in every raccoon.

Nor did I mind when, after I fed my furry pets all the treats they could eat, they repaid me by turning over countless foot-square sections of turf on the side lawn to search for grubs. It looked as if a shower of meteorites had plummeted into the grass during the night.

What concerned me was whether I could turn all the sods

over again before our landlord chanced along. But it was easy once I started, because you can repair a very moist lawn in half an hour with a turf-edger, finishing the job by wearing rubber boots and doing a soft-shoe shuffle up and down, side to side, frontwards and backwards, heel and toe, dos-à-dos, around and around, along the borders of each block, to join up the edges. (If some passing joggers thought my early-morning dance was amusing, I'd like them to know you can't do scientific restoration work like this by just plodding along.)

I've been impressed by the non-belligerence of most wild animals, compared with man. I'm sure our ten raccoons wouldn't bother with our German shepherd if he didn't want to tangle with them. As for Brutus, the cat, he races out to retrieve every marshmallow we throw to the raccoons, because he thinks they're his ping-pong balls. The raccoon always gets there first – and you should see the thunderstruck expression on Brutus' face when this strange creature sits up and actually *eats* his toy. But neither harms the other.

The worst my raccoon ever does, when a strange cat approaches his plate, is to stand up on his hind feet to full height and weave slowly from side to side in a menacing ritual, brandishing his front legs and stomping his feet – like an Apache war dance not going anywhere – as if to say, "I'm a vicious monster and something terrible is about to happen to you." This is supposed to psych the cat. It does.

Anyone can understand why the likable, irrepressible raccoon is the theme symbol of the Kindness Clubs, the organization launched by Mrs. Hugh John Flemming of Fredericton, New Brunswick, in a small local way a few years ago – and now a world-wide network of thousands of clubs and hundreds of thousands of members, a movement showing its most phenomenal growth in the new nations of Africa.

Whenever I do feel a little peeved at my pets, it's reassuring to think of Thornton W. Burgess, the famed Bedtime Story author of Hampden, Massachusetts. Although he came up to New Brunswick every year to fish, it was in the remote little West Indian island of Tobago that my wife and I met him on vacation visits. A cheery black maid would knock on the door of his little room every morning and say, "It's the hour to get to work!" and the aging author would start typing out his 15,000th daily story.

Later we used to drive down to his old-fashioned home in the rolling hardwood countryside of Hampden – when he was in his 90's and still writing – and he told us philosophically how the celebrated happy brook that wended past his home overflowed its banks in spring and inundated his living room. And the squirrels – no man had done so much to inculcate love for them – repaid him by burrowing under his eaves and wreaking thousands of dollars worth of damage on the house. Yet he wasn't angry.

As for embarrassments, I think again of Tobago. I brought a new pair of flower-patterned walking shorts and on impulse, wore them to dinner. I hated to face the gauntlet of some Canadian girls who loved to poke fun and disconcert me. Just as I passed their cottage, the strident wolf-whistles I had expected pierced the air. I walked faster and faster, trying not to panic – and arrived at the diningroom with my ears burning to find the girls already there. My commentator had been a Tobago bird – a cornbird, I think.

Then there was the Saint John department store that had a talking Mynah bird as the star of its pet section. One day I found a class of school girls there trying to get it to talk. I shouldered through the crowd and said, "Let *me* try." They made a path for me, and waited expectantly. "Hi, Peter, Peter, Peter," I exclaimed. Nothing happened. So I said his name in ingratiating baby-talk, which I felt sure would get results. *"Peetie – Peetie – Pete?"* The girls held their breath. He cocked his head and looked at me. *"Peetie – Peetie – Peetie?"* I repeated.

He stared again for a moment, then said out loud, in very plain English:

"You can't talk – Why don't you whistle?"

But people's interest in animals and birds, as I've indicated in this book, is tremendous and growing. I was never more impressed by it than when we were packing to leave Florida in early May to return to New Brunswick. A man came running out of the condominium building.

"My wife tells me you're a Canadian author. What do you write?" he asked.

"Oh," I said, "humorous pieces, history and travel, last time ghosts and pirates. . . . This week I spent two mornings at St. Petersburg Beach with the head trainer of the dolphins."

"Say! That would be something – I'm *interested* in them!"

"Well" – I tried to be unassuming – "dolphins are pretty wonderful; they're so intelligent."

"Are they ever!" he agreed. "More than half of them are college graduates!"

I looked at him closely.

"Are they really?"

"Oh yes! Why, I've lived in Tampa for years, but I've followed the Miami Dolphins ever since they started."

Not till then did I realize he was talking about a football team.

"And," he added with a laugh to show it was a humorous sally and he didn't really mean it, "we thought it was pretty sneaky of your Canadian city of Toronto to try to take three of them away from us!"

I laughed too, and we waved to each other as he left; but I didn't attempt to explain it, because packing is an awful job and my wife was staring at me impatiently.

The Beast
in the Dark

If you want to be the most popular person in your suburban neighbourhood – the subject of every conversation – there is no better way than to keep rabbits.

I found this out at Epworth Park on the St. John River when our first son was recovering from measles.

We bought a pair of white Angora rabbits so he could put his hand into the cage from his bed and pat the soft fluffy fur. They were very lovable with their snowy coats and pink eyes, nibbling on lettuce.

Immediately a different atmosphere became apparent in the community.

Neighbours who always took me for granted, who didn't even look up from their newspapers on the verandah when I walked by, all started staring at me. I think people admire those who do something different. Several who had never spoken to me before called out to me.

In fact, Sam Blackburn, who raises a big garden, even struck up a pleasant conversation. He said, "Are you planning to let those damn things run loose?"

"Oh, no," I said cheerily, "I'm keeping them under control!"

At that moment I was hippity-hopping past his front door trying to catch up with the bigger rabbit, which had escaped from the cage while I was putting its plate of food in. It was always one jump ahead of me and was about to dodge into Mr. Blackburn's lettuce patch.

"They're death on peas," said Sam Blackburn, following along behind me as if anxious to see if he could be of any assistance; I never knew he was so helpful. "But lettuce – Lord, they'll clean a patch of lettuce right out."

"I'll bet they would if they could," I said. "The little mischiefs!"

We cornered the rabbit between his toolsheds, and Sam Blackburn was good enough to walk all the way home with me, holding down the lid of the cardboard carton I was carrying, so the rabbit couldn't possibly get out again.

The very next day Walter Bollard, another amateur gardener whom I hardly knew even to speak to, wandered over past our cottage and inquired casually, "How long do you plan to keep those rabbits of yours?"

"Oh, I've no idea. Probably forever! Haven't even given it a thought yet."

His face fell. I think he was quite interested in having rabbits himself – he was probably hoping we'd sell them to him.

"Have there been any signs of – er – little rabbits appearing? They multiply like electronic calculators, you know."

This only proved what I thought – he wanted some rabbits.

"No," I laughed. I hated to disappoint him. "We've had our rabbits only a week. Give us time! And I don't even know whether they're a matched pair."

"But in any case, you're keeping them caged?"

"Of course. We're not letting them run around."

He was looking about as I spoke. "Well," he said, "I must get back to weeding my carrots and beans." He was peering at the empty cage on the verandah. "Where are those two rabbits right now, if I may ask?"

I laughed again.

"That's the funniest thing. Can you imagine? The little

devils got out of the cage door again when I was feeding them. Some people say rabbits are stupid, but I can tell you they're smart as a whip. They both hid under the verandah, just about a foot past where I can reach them without getting stuck!"

Mr. Bollard didn't think it was the funniest thing. Apparently he didn't see the point; I think he's slow-witted. He just hurried out, because his chores were on his mind.

I eventually got the rabbits back with offerings of lettuce – and a big salmon net.

It was the very next day that a group of neighbours, sort of a committee, called on us, and Mr. Blackburn was the spokesman.

"We'd like to see your son have a pet that would be a real companion," he said. "So we want to offer him a genuine purebred spaniel in exchange for the rabbits."

Wasn't that real neighbourliness? I never knew they thought so much of us.

But even though the rabbits were getting to be a lot of work for me – feeding them, chasing them, crawling under verandahs – I rather liked them. I asked the neighbours to let me think it over.

Then something happened that made up my mind.

My wife had undergone an operation in the city, and her sister from Moncton was looking after our son.

The rabbits were in their cage on the open back porch; I had carefully covered it over with mats for the night, and put big sticks of fireplace hardwood on top of the mats to hold them down.

You see, we don't have dangerous animals in the New Brunswick woods, just some animals that might be dangerous to rabbits – like foxes and wildcats or even eastern panthers, which I've never seen.

So I figured that after I built up layers of rugs and hardwood, if a wild creature tried to get at the rabbits in the darkness I'd hear the heavy sticks falling with loud clumping and I'd rush downstairs and save them.

At 2 A.M. I was startled out of my sleep by a tremendous THUMP!

It shook the cottage. It sounded as if a giant standing a few feet from the building had hurled a stick of hardwood at the wall.

THUMP!

Again the whole place trembled, and I jumped out of bed. I thought it was an earthquake.

I called down through the floorboards to my wife's sister in the bedroom below.

"Bernis, what on earth was *that?*"

Now, my wife's family grew up on a farm, and they knew about things.

"The rabbits," she called back.

"No – I mean the big *thump.*"

"It's the rabbits. They're thumping. It means 'Danger is near.' There must be a wild animal around."

Somewhere, I now remembered, I read that rabbits have great power like a coiled spring in their hind legs. But I never imagined they could make a house shake.

It took a lot of courage, I can tell you, to run down and face the wild animal – but I had to do it or lose our pets.

My heart pounding, I grabbed a flashlight, crept down the stairs, snatched a poker off the kitchen wood stove, snapped on the rear porch light, opened the door and rushed out, poker upraised high.

There, bathed in the glare of the lights, staring back at me, transfixed with fear, was – a little brown rabbit.

To the tame white Angoras under the mats, the visitor had a strange wild smell – thus the alarms.

I looked at the brown rabbit for a moment, then sighed and went into the kitchen. Like the house, I was shaken. I had been on a strict bland diet for twelve years, but I poured

16

myself a glass of my wife's cooking brandy.

Later that day I went back to the people we'd bought the rabbits from. They said they had other customers on a waiting list and they bought the rabbits back.

I suppose I could have sold them to some of our neighbours who were good enough to enquire about them, but at that moment I wanted to get rid of them completely.

After all, I told myself, they could buy their own rabbits.

But no one did.

How Little Cora
Became a Star

In the legend-rich Miramichi forests, lumberjacks tell me
with awe how clever the ravens are. I always thought they
were just king-size bluey-black super-crows, feathered
scavengers often seen along New Brunswick highways. But
the timber-cutters insist with straight faces that the ravens,
from their perches high in a white pine tree, can cock their
heads and see a man taking aim at them with a rifle and,
when he pulls the trigger, watch the bullet coming and
dodge it.

Cora is a raven – but for some reason she failed to dodge.

Her rustic home was near Caledonia Mountain. Unfortunately for her, robins were eating the crop on the large commercial blueberry fields near by. Local people were hired to
shoot the robins – and Cora, a partly grown raven, got in the
way.

Wounded in the wing, she would never be able to fly again,
even if she survived. No one at that moment would have
given two cents for her prospects in life.

Somebody carried the injured bird to Dr. Majka's home on

the mountain. There young Chris, only eleven, who loved pets, was only too happy to adopt her and look after her.

Incidentally, Caledonia is only a tiny mountain by world standards (1,200 feet), but it reminded the Majkas a little of Austria. Actually they are Polish, but they met after the Second World War in Austria, where both were medical students. They immigrated to Canada after graduation – first to Ontario, then to New Brunswick, where the father became a pathologist in the government laboratory in Moncton.

It was Chris who named Cora for *Corvus Corax,* her scientific species; he lavished raven delicacies on her (from dog food to dead mice), and she thrived. She lived in a spacious home-within-a-home – a big portable cage made out of metal screens – and hopped at will around the house. If she couldn't fly, she could at least flap her wings and jump up to a perch.

"We didn't attempt to train her," says Chris, now a summertime naturalist for the provincial government. "But we could see she was smart. She always looked fine and in good spirits. She knew her name, and when we talked to her she was very attentive and listened and watched everything. She croak-talked to other ravens."

Luckily, the Majka home had an affinity for wild creatures. Chris and his younger brother had brought up lizards and once even befriended a pair of infant seals rescued by two Paris journalists, via helicopter from the Atlantic ice floe massacre. The Majkas gladly took on the task of caring for the foundlings for a week. They shovelled snow into an improvised seal house. They got a recipe for a big batch of artificial seal's milk (four gallons of cream, a quart of cod liver oil, a quart of corn oil, half a dozen eggs, and other ingredients) so the babies could be fed every two or three hours. Eventually one seal went to the Brussels Zoo, the other to Monaco as a gift to Prince Rainier.

In the autumn, after Cora had been with the Majkas for

four months, a big local event took place – the annual Albert County Fair. Headlined as usual was Frank Weed and his wild life show, with wolves, a mountain lion, lizards, alligators, monkeys and all kinds of other wonderful things. This was to change the course of Cora's life.

Chris had often traded pets with Frank Weed, an American animal trainer who comes to the Maritime provinces so often he maintains a summer home at Cole's Island, New Brunswick, as well as a winter home at Fort Lauderdale.

Once Chris bartered away seven bats and, boy, do you know what he got? A real-live, three-foot-long iguana.

Now the youngster was asking Frank Weed whether he wanted any more bats or turtles or anything.

"What I'd really like to find this year," the animal trainer replied, "is a raven – a raven to train."

Chris said, "I have just the thing for you!"

So the boy traded his raven for two snakes – and Cora found herself to be no longer a humble country bird but a showgirl, a member of the entourage of the "Frank Weed Exotic Creature Show."

I didn't ask Chris what his long-patient mother thought when he excitedly brought home two snakes. He did mention, however, that one day a visitor got a shock when he looked up at the empty electric-light outlet in the ceiling and a snake came spiralling out of it.

The next summer, when Frank Weed came back, Chris asked, "How did that raven make out?"

The answer surprised him. Not only had the trainer taught Cora to respond to his voice – to stay in one place or jump up on a perch or squawk on command – but she could now say four or five words.

"And not long after that," continued Chris, "the Walt Disney people were looking for an intelligent raven to use in the movie series 'Gentle Ben,' and Frank Weed said, 'I have just the thing for you.' So Cora was featured on TV. Gentle Ben is a bear, and the raven was guiding him from one place to another."

"Are you certain," I asked, "it was really Cora?"

"Perfectly sure," he answered. "It looked just like Cora's smile around the corners of her bill."

He added happily, "We like to think that now she's probably bought a birdhouse in Beverly Hills and retired."

Some time after talking with Chris, I noticed a special section in the Saint John *Telegraph-Journal:*

Don't Miss It! There's Fun For Everyone At
The Sussex Fall Fair!

For the eighth year in a row, it heralded, the master of ceremonies would be none other than Frank Weed, the famous animal trainer.

We drove to Sussex early on the opening day – and found a personable, virile manager who looked like a white Stetson-hatted Western star and who answered our questions readily while responding to urgent queries from half a dozen fair officials tugging at his coat-tails at the same time.

"I think the raven and the crow are probably the smartest birds," he said, "smarter than the parrot or the mynah, which are the best talkers. A mynah has been known to learn a thousand words, a parrot rarely more than fifty."

He has trained everything from bobwhite quail, pheasants, grouse, Hungarian partridge and peacocks to wolves and snakes; but his favourite pupils are bobcats and mountain lions.

Running around loose in his Fort Lauderdale home at the same time have been pets as varied as a mountain lion, a wolf and an otter. "I always raise some animals in the house. They boss the dog."

What is his basic principle for training birds?

"Endless repetition," he said. "A bird on a string. No rewards, no punishment."

Never any chastising?

"Well . . . in the case of a rattlesnake, for example, when you hold out your arm and it strikes (its jaws are taped together), you give it a little slap. This goes on, oh, fifty times. Then the rattler doesn't react any more. You take off the tapes, offer your arm – and he does nothing."

Frank Weed frequently enjoys a morning cup of coffee in the company of his favourite rattler, Stanley. Matter of fact, he's so much at home with reptiles he's appeared in several movies with them, including the terror film *Stanley* and *The Death Curse of Tartu,* in which he played the role of Sam Benton, an explorer in the Everglades, who got crushed and suffocated by an anaconda. In *Frogs,* for a change, he was gulped down by an alligator. ("I was a double, and we used several alligators, with black tape over their jaws.") Another time he doubled for an actor who was ostensibly to be bitten by a rattler; for some reason nobody else wanted the job. His wife, in bit parts and as a double, shared some of his horror experiences. Understandably, Frank Weed is now very good at such Hollywood devices as holding his breath until his face turns blue, but he would rather die a more orthodox tragic death with tomato ketchup spurting from his mouth.

It should be noted that Frank Weed doesn't claim to be immortal. During a Scout Cub safety lecture, he was bitten through his boot by a water moccasin snake – a reverse illustration of safety measures. His wife Ellen sucked out the venom in time.

Naturally, a trainer this versatile is in demand for the filming of TV commercials.

For instance, Frank taught a crow to stand on a man's shoulders to make an ad for Crow light whiskey . . . a dove to alight beside a box of cottage cheese . . . a dog to point at a big bag of dog food (by happy chance, Frank Weed had put a quail inside).

But what about Cora the raven?

"She's fine," said Frank Weed. "She appeared in two epi-
sodes of 'Gentle Ben.' I'm fortunate to have three ravens
from New Brunswick at Fort Lauderdale, because you don't
find them farther down the Atlantic coast than Maine. And
they all talk."

"What does Cora say?"

"She says, 'How are you, Charlie?' "

The Dolphin
Who Came Home

Tom Haslett is modest about his dolphins and himself. Well groomed, informally dressed, with his styled dark hair and modern glasses, he looks at twenty-seven more like a college senior than a flamboyant showman.

The youthful chief trainer at the St. Petersburg Beach Aquatarium in Florida stands in awe of the intelligence of dolphins, often called "cousins of man." But he won't contend they're the smartest non-human creatures in the world. "Some people think they are," he says, "some think chimpanzees are, but I think they're in such totally different environments it's impossible to compare them."

Nor will he acknowledge there's anything special about his own talents as a trainer of six years' standing.

"Once dolphins are trained," he says, "it's only a matter of teaching a new trainer the right hand-signals. The animals (that's what he calls dolphins) will respond to anyone."

What he doesn't mention is that the big knack is in the original training of the dolphins – a task that calls for skill, ingenuity and experience, as well as infinite patience on the part of both teacher and pupil – and this is where he spends much of his time. Above all, the handler must know how far he can push the training, because if the dolphin becomes too

exasperated or weary, it may take a long while to get back to square one.

However, there is a definite claim Tom Haslett will make without much fear it can be disputed. Dolphins, he says, are surely the friendliest, gentlest and kindest wild creatures to be found anywhere. They seem to feel a glowing goodwill toward mankind – the way much of mankind feels only at Christmas.

They gambol and frolic among girl divers feeding them in the depths of the 100-foot-wide, 25-foot-deep, high-jumping aqua-theatre; they swim casually to the surface and stand up half out of the water looking with interest at the spectators looking at them; they do slow roll-overs and fancy turns as if showing off, all the time wearing the inerasable smile that Mother Nature in a happy mood engraved on the whole species.

"Some of them, like Duchess and Duffy, really seem to love people," says Haslett.

In fact, they are a lot like people. To begin with, they're mammals, not fish. They have to come up to breathe air every thirty or forty seconds. They are born like mammals, not hatched from eggs, and are nursed by their mother.

At the moment of birth, as the infant emerges tail-first, it's important to get the baby dolphin up to the surface quickly for its first gasp of air.

Tom Haslett speaks of his eleven dolphins sentimentally, like people he knows and loves: "When Thor arrived – the only animal ever born here – an old dolphin named Mabel acted as midwife. She assisted the mother, Floppy, and 'bumped' the baby up to the surface to start it breathing. Then she helped teach it to swim.

"Later, whenever Floppy did her twenty-five-foot jumps in the show – she and Casey always jumped together – little Thor would immediately dart over and stay with Mabel, then rush back to his mother when she returned."

(Dolphins incidentally have the ability to leap to incredible heights. Haslett says, "My brother, who is very dependable, told me he has seen these animals jump up fifty feet into the air out in the Gulf of Mexico.")

The "bumping up" procedure at birth, the trainer believes, may account for the myriad tales that have come down to us from antiquity about dolphins saving the lives of drowning fishermen and sailors by pushing them to shore. Crashed pilots in the Second World War told of being boosted along through the waves by dolphins.

"It's possible this is how the animals instinctively react when they find a helpless creature in the water," he says. "They seem to have a special affinity for humans."

And speaking of mild dispositions: When being netted out in the Gulf of Mexico by Aquatarium personnel, at first the dolphins naturally try to escape. When they realize they're captured, they don't exhaust themselves by uselessly threshing about and flailing their tails at anyone who comes near. Instead they become quiet, as if conserving their strength to see what's going to happen.

But don't think for a moment they're submissive creatures who believe in always turning the other cheek. "No known attack has ever been made by a dolphin on a human being," says the trainer. "However, if a shark is threatening young dolphins or a sick dolphin, that's different." Amazingly, this smaller denizen of the deep (the average dolphin is seven to eight feet long, 350 to 400 pounds) can knock out a marauding man-eating shark armed with ferocious teeth and gaping jaws – knock him out so fast the shark never knows what hit him.

Racing at high speed, the dolphin smashes into the shark's soft body with a snout fortified by a rock-hard protruding lower jaw – a terrific impact that causes the enemy's vital organs to rupture and haemorrhage. For good measure, the dolphin administers the marine version of the old one-two punch. It whiplashes the shark with its powerful tail, a blow of such force it sometimes lifts the dying predator right out of the water.

We caught a glimpse of this power while viewing the dolphin and sea lion show in the adjoining Gold Dome aquatheatre. Dolphins were throwing baseballs at their trainers in a simulated big-league pitcher-batter duel, and scoring actual baskets by tossing basketballs. Star performer Cher demonstrated how she can head-butt a soccer ball accurately – and then "kicked" the ball with a lash of her tail, sending it soaring right up through the open roof of the amphitheatre and far out of sight!

With fearsome capabilities like that, you'd think a dolphin might react fiercely if he was slapped by a human trainer.

"The only time I ever became annoyed with our animals," recalls Haslett ruefully, "was during underwater training when one kept bumping my hand repeatedly to try to get a fish I was holding. Without thinking, I swatted him – not hard; it didn't hurt.

"He just looked at me in disbelief, as if to say, 'You must be crazy!' I felt terrible afterward, the compassionate way he was looking at me. I never did it again."

We asked, "Did the dolphin do it again? Did he stop butting your hand?"

Tom Haslett grinned. "No, he didn't stop. I guess he couldn't realize I really meant it."

It's little wonder dolphins seem to like the companionship of children, because children are the humans they're most like. They love to play. Sometimes, out in the Gulf of Mexico, they've been seen tossing fish to one another in an impromptu game of catch – a sign they've had a good feed first.

Unexpectedly we got an inkling of this happy-go-lucky friskiness under the Golden Dome – not during the show but after it.

A rubber "baseball" being used in the pitcher-batter duel got away from the trainer and bounced to Cher, a non-player standing up treading water and impatiently watching from a small water-tank near by. Cher was elated. She hurled the ball into the air, caught it, did somersaults in the water. For the moment, they let her have it.

As the spectators trooped down the stairs after the performance, the trainer walked over and said quietly, "Come on, now, Cher – give me the ball."

She enjoyed this immensely. Swimming over to him, she held up the ball in her mouth, seeming to put it almost in his hands, but the moment he made a move she dived again, only to re-emerge a moment later and offer it repeatedly – temptingly and tantalizingly.

"It's like a pup playing," my wife whispered. "She's saying, 'I've got the ball and you haven't.' "

People stopped exiting to watch.

Another trainer came along and suggested offering the dolphin a soccer ball as a trade. Cher was having none of it. She held up the baseball to both of them in turn, challenging them.

The man who had given the show's running commentary over the public address system climbed back up the stairs to his booth. He was laughing. Over the air rasped his voice:

"Cher – please don't tease the trainers."

We never found out how it ended.

But if dolphins are like playful kids, they're like good kids, too. They try to learn, try to grasp what the four trainers at the Aquatarium are asking them to do.

"If they can't understand, if they feel frustrated, they'll show it by snapping their tails or blowing air bubbles under water," says Haslett. "Then they'll go away and stay with the other animals for a while, and when they come back they'll be refreshed and able to try again better.

"It's often helpful to put them in with older animals

already trained. They may not catch on to the 'behaviours' (stunts) by just watching, but they lose their fear of the props used in the acts – hoops, plastic batons, basketballs, ropes.

"Like mischievous youngsters with a new school teacher, they'll test a new handler to find out how far they can go. They know who's who, and they respond a little differently to a new trainer. For instance, they may not jump quite so high as usual.

"Sometimes, if they've already eaten their fill, they'll balk altogether at doing certain behaviours." In other words, as the dolphins see the unassailable logic of it, why should they work for a tossed fish if they're already full?

The training of a dolphin is a fascinating blend of (1) the repetition-and-reward system of teaching tricks that the trainer wants his charges to do; and (2) the cultivation of unusual traits shown by individual dolphins in order to create unusual "behaviours."

We asked Tom Haslett about a show-stopper – Casey's backward dance, a skittering perpendicular shimmy while standing on his tail in the water, from the trainer right across the wide tank. It's rapid action – something like a paint-mixing machine shaking up a can of paint in a hardware store.

Was this a natural habit of dolphins at sea? Or a peculiarity of Casey himself? Or something deliberately taught?

The trainer was nodding.

"You mean Casey's tail-walk – what the announcer calls the 'Dolphin Boogaloo.' It's natural to a degree, but mostly taught.

"When the trainer is about to throw a fish, the dolphin comes up out of the water. You throw it a little over his head and he quickly backtracks to catch it. Each time you throw it back farther, and he tail-walks farther back in anticipation. Finally he gets to know it's expected of him, and he does it as a matter of course."

We were strolling out to the children's dolphin pool, known

as the kidney pool because of its shape. One of the two dolphins was partly out of the water and being patted on his shining wet head – a texture like the grey rubber suit worn by a diver – by an eager group of boys about eleven or twelve.

"Yes, they're like people," Tom Haslett was saying. "They're even subject to people diseases. Mabel, the old midwife, died of a heart attack. Another died of pancreatitis. And pneumonia is always a hazard.

"The one I felt worst about was our baby, Thor. He died at two years, and the autopsy showed it was poison. We had scientists make every conceivable test – they even tested leaves that might have fallen from nearby trees – but without result." He was pensively silent for a few moments. "It took me a long while to get over that." You didn't have to look at his downcast face to believe him.

Every dolphin, it transpired, has his own personality, his own idiosyncrasies, his own voice.

"It's like fingerprints," explains Tom Haslett. "The clicks and whistles he emits – some beyond the range of human hearing – are distinctive to him alone. They say to the other dolphins, 'I'm Joe Blow.' "

The recent scientific experimental work with these animals has launched a new wave of public interest in dolphins. All marine theatres are noticing this. It's not only kids now who are coming to watch an entertaining show; adults come, too, thousands of them, wanting to make their own evaluation of the dolphin by watching him perform at close range.

Contributing to the upsurge of public attention are the sporadic rumours out of Washington about U.S. Navy projects exploiting the military uses of dolphins – uses reportedly as varied as detecting enemy mines, locating air crashes, retrieving lost missiles, tracking ships, attaching explosives to hulls in enemy harbours.

But the Navy, which occasionally buys dolphins from

aqua-theatres, never divulges how well they are performing – or what their new stunts are.

Will man some day be able to communicate directly with dolphins?

"That's one of many questions that still await answers," replies Tom Haslett. "I'm sure that dolphins can warn each other. But whether they can communicate across hundreds or even thousands of miles, as some investigators claim, well, I would question it.

"There's no doubt about their intelligence. They have a brain bigger than man, but of course part of it is for their sonar – the echo-locating signals they send out and receive. We know from experiments, for instance, that a dolphin in the dark can tell the difference between two metal plates of different sizes. But research is really only beginning. No one even knows yet how fast a dolphin is capable of travelling in the open sea."

What's a fully-trained dolphin worth on the selling market today?

The trainer pondered. "I've heard of one or two performing animals being leased out with a trainer for three to six months for as much as $50,000."

While we talked, I was dropping silvery fish into the waiting maw of the same dolphin the kids had patted earlier. (A booth sells paper cups containing a few sardine-sized fish for twenty-five cents; but in bringing them back to the dolphin pool I had to run a gauntlet of the performing sea lions' runs. They knew what was in the paper cups and kept up an insistent "oink"-barking – *"oink, oink, oink, oink!"* – until I threw them some, too.)

"Didn't a research expert say the other day," I enquired, "that dolphins shouldn't be kept in captivity too long? That years of confinement in tanks can frustrate them beyond endurance?"

Haslett shrugged, frowning earnestly. "Any animals I've known always seemed happy; they always seemed to enjoy what they did."

Though I didn't realize it at the moment, a more tangible answer – a convincing real-life answer – was only a foot away from me. It was just under my extended hand as I fed the dolphin.

That answer came to light a moment later.

"These two dolphins in the children's pool," I said, "are they young ones that haven't been trained yet?"

"Oh no, the dolphin you're feeding, Pete, is one of our older animals."

"Then can't he be used as a performer in the shows?"

"It's not exactly that," Tom Haslett said – and he related an extraordinary story:

Pete was captured in a net years ago in the Gulf of Mexico. When they brought him ashore, he was found to have several bad shark-bite scars.

"One wound," recalls Haslett, "had the effect of ruining his masculinity, his manhood. We thought it was a shame, to keep and train a maimed dolphin; so eventually, after using him as a 'feeder' animal for some months in the children's pool, we took him out again and released him into the gulf.

"The strange thing was, we caught him again on a subsequent trip."

"Wouldn't the mathematical chances against that be astronomical?"

"Oh yes, it was unusual, because the gulf is thousands of square miles in size. We let him go.

"Later we found him in our net again. This was astonishing, because dolphins are so intelligent they even seem to know the pitch of our boat engine. They swim around excursion boats, and follow them and keep up with them, but when they hear us coming – *zap!* – they're gone, just like that.

"The third time we looked in our net and found Pete, we

began to realize that instead of running away he was following our boat so he could get caught. After all, he might be still afraid of sharks – no doubt he had been attacked when he was young, or not well one day, or taken by surprise. And he might have felt that out in the gulf he was no use – he couldn't reproduce – so he wanted to come back to the children at the Aquatarium, where he had been happy.

"What settled it in our minds was when we held the net open for him to get away. Any other dolphin would vanish in a wink, but Pete stayed in the net. He didn't want to escape. So we brought him home again with us, and here he is."

Pete was sitting up in front of me, smiling, waiting for another treat. For some reason I walked all the way back past the sea lions to the booth and bought him more fish.

What you notice most about Tom Haslett is that he speaks enthusiastically of other dolphin shows around the United States and Canada. In this highly competitive world, whether in sports or entertainment or anything else, you normally expect one participant to speak at best with grudging approval of another.

Not in dolphin-training, it seems. When I mentioned a Florida show where a trainer travels around the tank standing on the backs of two harnessed dolphins, and another trainer rides astride a killer whale as it leaps and dives, Haslett's face lit up.

"They're great acts," he declared. "Those behaviours take a lot of training."

No two dolphin shows are exactly alike, for that matter. At St. Petersburg Beach, for instance, they do a unique behaviour in the high-jumping aqua-theatre. Three dolphins come soaring up at the same time to take fish from the trainer standing in the bucket of the elevated crane. One takes a fish from his left hand, one from his right, one from his mouth.

If there's any dolphin that Haslett doesn't admire – remote as that possibility may seem – it's the fresh-water variety.

"You've never seen one?" he asked, his face wrinkling painfully at the thought. "Well, just let me say it's not the prettiest sight in the world, with its little ratty eyes and ugly face."

But his own animals, the salt-water dolphins, are something else. To him they're beautiful – even though the dictionary calls them Atlantic "bottle-nose" dolphins, and first-time spectators sometimes draw back in dismay when they see the hole in their head where they blow out geysers of air.

You see, as a boy growing up, Tom Haslett had no pets. Other boys had dogs or cats or squirrels. But Tom could only look on, and wish, at his inland home in Bartow – because his mother was allergic to dust from animal fur.

Now he's making up for lost time. He has a life filled with pets.

"You can't work with these animals," he says, "without feeling affection for them. Whenever I go on vacation, I see all the dolphin shows I can – not because I miss them, you realize, but because I like to see what other trainers are doing."

"That's understandable."

He sighs a little, looking down at Pete's smile that just won't come off.

"They're such a beautiful animal, aren't they? So pleasant to look at. . . ."

And after spending a few hours with Tom Haslett, and patting and feeding Pete, the Dolphin Who Came Home, you have to agree.

In the marine world, these *are* the beautiful people.

It's Easy
to Banish Raccoons

One of the nice things about having a pet is that it reminds a man how superior he is in every way to God's lower creatures.

Look at our raccoons. Was it ever fun to humour them by carrying out the left-over supper scraps on an old silver foil dinner plate – just as though the little tykes were special guests – and leaving the shining plate, piled with chunks of fish and potatoes, by the entrance to their home under the garage!

But do you know what those nervy raccoons did? They thought they were entitled to VIP treatment – and the dinnerware, too.

In the morning the food was gone and the silver foil platter as well. They'd pulled it under the garage and kept it.

Mrs. Moriarty, who was helping us houseclean that spring, sniffed, "Now they can eat all their meals off silver dishes."

I became smarter.

Next time I heaped the scraps on another foil plate, carried it out, but didn't leave it. I just held the plate down low in my hands, with the rim under the opening, and chirruped excitedly, *"Oh, look, look, look, look!,"* which always brought Smokey's wary head out to see the treat.

As expected, a black nose appeared from under the shingled wall. A paw that looked like a hand reached out and picked up a morsel of fish and put it into the mouth. I decided to wait until Smokey had cleaned off the entire plate, then take it back to use another day.

Suddenly the plate began to move away from me into the opening. Smokey was holding the other side in her paws, and pulling.

I grasped my side of the plate tight, and pulled back.

The plate slowly kept going away.

Frantically I braced myself and pulled with all my might.

But Smokey must have been bracing her feet too – she must have had a natural pulley of some sort, because any fool knows a raccoon has only small legs and can't compare in physique or strength with a grown man, particularly when it's only a little mother raccoon.

I had to let go. My edge of the plate vanished.

Mrs. Moriarty sniffed, but didn't say anything.

The following day I talked with a friend, Hank, who lives two miles away at East Riverside, about my experience. He was very encouraging. Somehow he got the idea I wanted to get rid of Smokey.

"I can tell you how to deal with raccoons," he said brightly. "Someone gave me a sack of fresh fish – gaspereaux – that I didn't want, so I had an inspiration: I would use them for fertilizer in my garden. I planted one potato, one gaspereau, one potato, one gaspereau – you see what I mean?

"Next morning the garden was all dug up. Raccoons love fish."

"But" – in surprise – "I thought you said you were going to tell me – "

"Just a moment: In the evening, I sat on a stool by the open bathroom window with a .22 rifle across my knees, waiting for that raccoon."

My spirits sank, for I hate to hear of wild life being harmed.

"You shot it?"

"No, I fell asleep and fell off the stool, and hurt my ribs."

"But – "

"Just a moment. Next morning a neighbour put me on the right track at last. He said, 'You don't need to shoot anything. There's one sure way to chase raccoons: Get a small transistor radio, tune in to one of those all-night rock music stations, turn it up loud, put it out in the middle of your garden, and that will frighten the raccoons away!' So I took his advice last night.

"I had my own transistor radio. I put it on the loudest-blasting station on the dial, turned it up good, and I placed the radio in a plastic bag to keep the weather off, and suspended it from a little stick in the garden."

"And it worked?"

He looked sad.

"In the morning it was gone. . . . The raccoons took it."

I wasn't sure what he thought the result of the experiment showed, but I didn't like to press him any more.

Later, back home, Mrs. Moriarty told me what the result showed.

"Now," she sniffed, "the raccoons can eat all their meals off silver plates and have a dance afterward."

The Day
the Bull Moose
Dropped In

One morning my elder son, hunting deer in the New Brunswick woods, heard a thunderous crashing – nearer and nearer.

Then he saw huge antlers bursting through the alder bushes: It was a bull moose!

"Next thing I knew," he said, "I was up a spruce tree and my rifle was on the ground. I don't know how I got there."

The moose snorted and pawed around for a while, then left.

It sent a shivery chill up my spine just to listen.

My wife, glancing over at my expression, commented, "I hate to think how *you'd* react. You'd be so petrified you'd never get out of the moose's way."

I could only nod, with another shudder.

Which only shows how little we know each other – and even ourselves.

On a crisp October morning, shortly afterward, I strolled down our driveway in Rothesay with briefcase under my arm, along the sidewalk to the bus stop.

I was early, and it was pleasant just to stand there and drink in the heady air and see the countryside so sharply delineated in the fall sunshine.

Idly looking up toward Philip Oland's grassy paddock –

where later in the day about two dozen riding horses and Shetland ponies and a donkey would be browsing – I didn't even raise an eyebrow when I saw a very tall gangling horse meandering across. It walked awkwardly, like a horse on stilts, with a long straggly black beard hanging down from its chin and towering many-branched horns above its head.

At the same instant that I realized it was a bull moose, I was seized by panicky fear – not for myself, but for the moose.

It was heading for the front door of the Oland residence. What if it continued down the driveway to the suburban highway? Wouldn't the next car be sure to hit it? Cars were always colliding with deer or moose in New Brunswick. Then it would have to be shot.

To my dismay the great animal turned right at the Olands' steps and started down the gravelled drive toward me, his pronged antlers riffling the lower maple branches.

Before I knew it, I had stepped forward to the edge of the pavement. I waved my briefcase up at the advancing moose.

"Go back!" I roared. "Go back!"

The moose stopped at the other side of the road; he shook his head from side to side as if he was trying to shake something off (or, as it appeared to me at the time, saying "No" emphatically).

In desperation I remembered how my father-in-law on the farm ordered his horses to back up. I shouted in urgent clipped tones with machine-gun speed:

"Bick! Bick! Bick! Bick! Bick!"

The moose just shook his huge head, the beard dancing like a Highlander's sporran.

While this tableau continued – the moose and I looking at each other from opposite sides of the road – several cars came along that ordinarily would have offered me a lift to town.

But it was a funny thing: No one did. Every car crept by at five miles an hour, the driver doing a double-take as he swivelled his head from one side to the other – then he stepped on the gas and bolted as if he'd just thought of something.

The moose swung left and started loping toward Saint John, ten miles away. Thank goodness, he was staying on the grassy border.

I walked down the middle of the road, waving the briefcase at him and hollering:

"Get out of here! Go 'way! *Git! Git! Git!*"

To my horror, the moose turned and ambled right out on the highway in front of me, walking toward the city at a leisurely plodding pace, straddling the middle line.

Certain he would be smashed by the first car coming up behind us, I walked down the road about thirty feet back of him, both arms stretched out to the sides like a traffic cop.

In the anguish of the moment, it seemed a sensible idea – car drivers were always hitting moose, but they wouldn't be so apt to hit a moose if they had to hit a human being first.

So a strange parade was seen wending its way down a country road like an impromptu circus, the moose's high rump undulating above me like the rear end of an elephant.

I kept hoping the moose would make a dash for the woods – but he seemed content to play he was a traffic vehicle. For some reason, as I walked and signalled, I wondered what they call that attendant in India who walks behind the elephant with a guide-stick in his hands. Is it an "oompah"? Or is that the sound made by a German band?

A hundred yards farther, down an incline, just opposite Dr. Maddison's house, the procession came to a sudden stop.

Facing the moose was a small red propane gas truck coming out from the city. Both halted.

I started backtracking, faster and faster, as I sensed the moose might wheel around.

It happened, just as I began sprinting up the rise, retracing my steps – he swerved about with a mighty heave of his hips.

43

Nearing the top, I looked back over my shoulder. The galloping beast was gaining fast.

A few yards more – and there was George B. Oland's driveway, on the opposite side of the road from son Philip Oland's, offering a ready escape route down to the shores of the broad Kennebecasis River.

Stopping in mid-road, I pivoted and, again like a traffic cop, facing the moose, held my left arm high and pointed sideways with my right arm, briefcase still in hand, shouting, "Down here! Down *here!*"

Incredibly, the bull moose followed traffic instructions like an experienced driver.

He leaned at a sharp angle to make the turn into the driveway. It reminded me more than anything of the world speed-skating meet I saw in Saint John as a teenager in 1926, when heavy-muscled hometown hero Charles I. Gorman, with thighs that looked to a skinny schoolboy as if they belonged to a draft horse, led the herd of flashing silver blades around the final turn of the 440-yard event in a tumult of clattering, thundering din.

The moose vanished down the slope to the river, his hoof-beats fading into nothingness.

All this had happened within the space of a few minutes.

I heard the bus approaching.

With a sigh, exhausted but strangely exhilarated, I flopped down into a seat beside an old friend, Hector McDade, a veteran deer and moose hunter. Too late I remembered, after I began pouring out my story, that Hector is also a notorious emotion-rouser. He can wring remorseful tears from a dockyard gang just by relating in poignant detail the death of his pet butterfly.

"Oh, my God!" he cried. "Don't tell me you stood right out there in broad daylight with a bull moose. You could have been killed!"

"He wasn't belligerent," I hurriedly explained. "I wasn't

44

invading his domain. He was just a poor bewildered forest creature looking for guidance to get back home."

"But this is the *rutting* season!" he agonized in high-pitched tones. He clasped his forehead in disbelief. "Bull moose are very temperamental – terribly irrational. When they're looking for a mate, they'll charge anyone!"

I was feeling less exhilarated all the time.

Helplessly I argued, "I knew there was a house thirty feet back of me – I could have dived through the window."

Hector McDade shook his head, inconsolable.

"You'd never have made it! Those gigantic hooves – a thousand pounds of heft behind them – half a ton – boy, they'd have mashed you up into mincemeat in twenty seconds flat. Lord above, you were lucky to escape in one piece. Oh, but you'll feel the reaction . . . you'll get an awful reaction any minute now!"

I could feel a pain coming under my rib cage.

Hector pondered and added, "Of course you'll get no credit for trying to save the moose, anyway – you know that! You realize Philip Oland and George Oland make Moosehead ale? Tell your experience and people will say it was either a tall horse story or an advertising gimmick."

I was getting off the bus in town then. He bade me a melancholy goodbye. "And to think, you would have left a wife and two kids. Were you lucky! But I hope you don't get too bad a reaction. . . ."

Strange: Whereas I had got on the bus only twenty minutes ago feeling fine, if keyed up, now I felt an increasingly acute pain in my stomach.

By the time I got to the office, a few blocks away, I was doubled up in abdominal distress.

But I didn't blame my friendly bull moose.

I blamed Hector McDade.

The Bird
That Sang Off-Key

Did you ever know that wild parakeets can be trained to talk just like parrots?

It's amazing. These beautiful little birds, no bigger than canaries, iridescent in green and blue and yellow hues, flit freely about the trees in Florida and less freely in cages in northern department stores under signs that say: "Special This Week – Budgies $5.95."

I heard that Mrs. Nada Jones at Seminole Palm Banks had enjoyed great luck in teaching parakeets to talk, so I asked her if we could visit her home and listen to one.

She was delighted. A plump, motherly woman who loves dumb creatures, she gave me a warm welcome.

On her back lawn were several bird-houses, sitting on top of six-foot poles.

"If you want to learn about parakeets," said Mrs. Jones, "you've come to the right place. Just watch!"

She ambled over the lawn and looked up to the front door of a birdhouse. She chortled: "Tweetie, tweetie, tweetie!"

Out of the tiny doorway squeezed a fat little blue-green bird, followed by another. Both sat on the porch platform, looking down at her intently.

"See?" she whispered. "They love me."

I didn't get that impression. They thought she was going to

feed them. Or possibly the male wanted his mate to see close-up the curious creature that lived in the big birdhouse.

"And now," she said excitedly, leading the way into the livingroom, "come and meet Pepe!"

With a proud wave of her hand she directed our gaze toward a cage in which a yellow and blue budgie sat silently swinging on a wooden perch. A brown spaniel was eyeing us from a corner of the room. In the opposite corner sat a man reading the paper; evidently it was Mr. Jones.

"Just listen to Pepe!" she went on. "Every parakeet we've given away – all over North America – has turned out to be a good talker. The males are the talkers; they have a touch of brown over their bills. But Pepe – he's the best, aren't you, dear?"

Pepe continued to swing, paying no attention.

Mrs. Jones prompted him: "Hello, hello, hello. . . . I'm a very happy little bird!"

Pepe, swaying, glanced down. He appeared only mildly interested in hearing how she felt.

"That's the trouble," Nada Jones commented. "It's always like this when you want him to perform. Perhaps he'll speak to the dog: *Oh, my, see Puff-Puff!*"

Nothing.

Sighing, Mr. Jones got up from his armchair and stiffly plodded over. He looked up at the bird as if it was a cross he had to bear.

"How are *you*, Pepe?" – ingratiatingly, hopefully.

No answer.

"How *are* you, Pepe?" – with a vicious inflection, as if he'd like to seize the bird in his hands and squeeze out a few words.

No response.

Mr. Jones plodded back, picked up the paper, slumped into the chair.

Just as we were about to take our leave, apologetically

agreeing life is always like that, we heard a radio program coming from the faint distance. It sounded like several men talking in the engine room of a ship. You could hear different voices, but in a subdued burbling chorus – too far away to catch the words.

Incredibly, it was Pepe.

The parakeet was playing back a radio drama he had heard and automatically preserved on his natural tape recorder.

Once started, Pepe was not to be denied his chance to shine.

"Poor Puff-Puff!" he said, in a voice surprisingly loud for a tiny bird.

"That's our dog," explained Nada Jones. "Not the dog talking – it's Pepe talking about the dog."

"Yes," I said. "I gathered that."

"Holy biddy," said the voice. "Hot damn!"

"That's something he learned from the cleaning-woman," Mrs. Jones hastily pointed out.

In a quick change of pace, the bird began a flat-voiced chant:

"Help us love you,
    In all things one."

Exclaimed Mrs. Jones, "Isn't that lovely! He knows a lot of religious passages."

As if encouraged, Pepe shrilled:

"Hear, oh hear, your loving children's prayer."

Then he added: "Holy biddy! Damn the torpedoes! Poor Puff-Puff." To top it off, he gave with remarkable trueness the musical chime notes of Avon Calling.

"Well," I said quickly, wanting to get out while there was still time, "we've really heard a parakeet talk, so thanks very much and. . . ."

"Oh, but you haven't heard him sing – that's *something*. You'll want to wait!"

49

Her husband was glaring over the top of his paper as if hoping we wouldn't want to wait.

Pepe interrupted in masculine tones: "This meal is vile!" It was strange, because he wasn't even eating. "Woman, you're a rotten cook."

Nada Jones hurriedly interjected, "Oh! The terrible things he learned from that cleaning-woman."

The bird perked up again.

"Pray for us sinners now and at the hour of our death."

"That's more like it," said Mrs. Jones approvingly with relief. "He learned that from me."

Now a bird voice came that sounded peculiarly like Nada Jones herself, talking to somebody.

"Aren't you *ever* going to take a bath?"

"Isn't that cute!" she intervened quickly. "Him wants his iddy bird bath."

I was going to say how much it sounded like her voice, but my wife's elbow nudged me in the ribs.

Just as quickly Mrs. Jones added: "Show the nice man and womie how you can sing, Pepe! I taught him the national anthem myself. Now, I'll start the words: Oh say. . . ."

The bird regarded her blankly.

"Oh say, can you see. . . ." she chanted in a toneless voice.

Abruptly Pepe burst into song – but what an eerie ear for music! It sounded like the words of the "Star Spangled Banner," but set to a new discordant tune.

Instead of the familiar cadence:

```
                              by
                  see    the              light
     Oh-          you          dawn's   ly
         oh    can                    ear-
              say
```

– he sang in monotonous sing-song disharmony:

<pre>
                say   you   by   dawn's   light –"
    "Oh oh   can   see   the   early
</pre>

It was horrible. It was completely disenchanting. It proved to me that parakeets, remarkable mimics as they are, can't even carry three notes of a tune.

Mrs. Jones was ecstatic.

"Did you hear that? He sang a whole stanza! Wasn't that smart?"

As if to show he was even smarter, Pepe said reproachfully in an unmistakably feminine voice:

"You never give me *one thin dime* to spend on myself."

"Hush," she reprimanded in shocked tones, red-faced. "Forget what that awful cleaning-woman taught you. Now sing it for me once again, sing our national anthem. Oh say. . . ."

The bird kept mum.

"Oh say," she reiterated expectantly.

No response.

In an all-out final effort, she tried to prime him by singing it herself:

<pre>
                say   you   by   dawn's   light –"
    "Oh oh   can   see   the   early
</pre>

It was exactly the same hopelessly tuneless tune the parakeet had sung!

As we were leaving, Mrs. Jones beamed, "Well, I hope you learned something about parakeets."

"Yes, I certainly did," I assured her.

I learned that parakeets can sing, but she can't.

Tales of
Ten Raccoons

My first glimpse of our raccoons was one evening at twilight. I walked around the house and came upon three of them eating breadcrusts from a platter put out on the back lawn for the birds.

They evaporated instantly. They disappeared so fast into the small opening under the corner of the garage, it was as if you poured left-over coffee from several cups into a sink drain – *swirl* – *gone* – just like that.

I was sorry to think I'd given them such a scare. I knew they wouldn't re-appear for a long time, if ever. I might never see wild raccoons at close hand again.

A minute later I looked out the kitchen window – and there they were, the three of them, out on the back lawn eating again as if nothing had happened.

So I went out the front door, walked around quietly. In an attempt to set them at ease, I said as I turned the corner, "Hello, Mr. Raccoon. Think it looks like a nice day tomorrow?" They retreated again, but not so fast.

As an experiment, I kept doing this.

Soon they were paying no attention whatsoever to me.

They regarded me as a nonentity, a genial eccentric who couldn't make up his mind about the weather.

Then I began to get concerned – our ninety-pound German shepherd Fritz in daytime shared a garage wall with the raccoons. (There was space enough under the garage for them to emerge at will, but not enough for him to squeeze through.) I took Fritz out on the leash late at night, and when he saw the raccoons on the lawn he nearly carried me along like a kite flying behind him, he was so eager to get at them.

The dog was quivering all over, even after they had vanished, and I could see a disastrous battle might be coming. It was no use – I had to un-tame my raccoons as soon as possible and make them stay away.

The next time I took Fritz out – much as I hated to do this to the raccoons – I ran him growling over to the hole under the garage, and lambasted the shingles loudly with a baseball bat, *Whack! Wham! Wham!*, shouting, "Get out of here! Get out for good!"

I hated to do it, as I said, because the raccoons, terrified out of their wits, might never emerge again. They might starve to death in there.

Then I led the dog over, as usual, to a tall tree on the fringe of the woods. When I looked back over my shoulder, the three raccoons were sitting on the lawn outside the hole, watching us with interest.

We walked back to the kitchen door; the bold trio didn't move. The dog stiffened at the sight of them, reared up on the leash and, roaring, plunged toward them, only to be yanked back. They didn't even budge. They knew he was restrained. They could see the shining leash. They knew he couldn't move any faster than I could.

So I gave up trying to scare them away. I resigned myself to the hope there would never be a direct confrontation, and decided to re-tame them.

If the raccoons were surprised to see the bellowing, bat-swinging eccentric suddenly become friendly again, they gave no sign. Apparently they take the strange human species as they find them, day by day.

A few weeks later one of the three raccoons wandered away, leaving just two, who were evidently mates. One of our granddaughters named them – the male, the smaller and aggressive one, became Smokey, and the female, the big over-plump booby that always hung back near the hole under the garage, became Cindy.

Smokey was wonderfully protective of his fat mate. Whenever you were feeding Smokey on the back driveway, he always kept a line of retreat open to that all-important entrance to his home.

If you walked rapidly sideways, trying to circumvent his stonewall defence, he'd hop sideways just as fast, like a kangaroo, to keep in front of you.

If you tried to make an end run around him, in order to feed the apprehensive big gump peeking out the hole, Smokey would race back to beat you to the opening, turn around quickly and block the hole with his backside half in it.

I said to my wife, "Isn't that wonderful! Instinctively he's protecting his mate."

Later, two things dawned on us.

One was the possibility that Smokey, in bravely blockading the hole, was only trying to prevent his mate from getting any of the treats.

The other – an astounding discovery my wife made – was that Smokey wasn't a male at all, but the female! The male, of all people, was Cindy, the big fat goop who would hardly venture out of the hole.

You couldn't help liking Smokey. For all her forwardness, she had a lovely personality. When you offered her food, she didn't snatch it and turn away, like some raccoons; nor did she even take it in her paws. Instead, she stood up on her hind legs and waddled over to you, her hand-like paws held out to both sides as if she were going to sing "Mammy," and opened her mouth for you to put the morsel in. Only then did she gently close her paws around it.

Smokey became as faithful as a dog. Any hour of the evening I could say to visitors, "Would you like to see my pet raccoon?" I'd snap on the back-door light – and there she would be, patiently sitting at the corner of the garage facing the kitchen window, her head nodding or sometimes drooping down on her chest.

I learned what she liked best – anything sweet, especially marshmallows, honey, peanut butter, molasses.

When I gave her a soda biscuit covered with peanut butter, she would assiduously lick off every trace of the spread until there was nothing left but a gleaming varnished biscuit; then she would look it over, study it, and finally eat it.

Smokey had a definite pecking order where food was concerned. Give her at the same time a honey-covered soda cracker, a dog biscuit, and a crust of bread – and she would eat them in that sequence.

I let her have only one marshmallow a day, I should point out. Everyone fretted that I might lavish too many on her. Even the supermarket manager who sold me the marshmallows asked me to go easy: "You don't want to turn her into a juvenile delinquent."

They needn't have worried. Smokey was getting a balanced diet. The dog treats alone – and she was doing away with as many as the dog – contained among other things: wheat flour, oat flour, soy flour, meat meal, dried whole eggs, dried skimmed milk, animal fat, bone meal, cheese meal, fish meal, alfalfa meal, not to mention several vitamin supplements.

Now she began venturing into the back porch when I hooked the screen door open, and she seemed perfectly at home. While I was getting her treats, she would stretch her front paws away out until her face was almost on the tile floor, yawn and show all her teeth and arch her neck away up, then stretch her hind legs out, dog fashion, one by one.

Given a big white marshmallow, Smokey would sit up as unashamedly unladylike as a Billingsgate Market fishwife, her two hind legs spread out on the floor at right angles in front of her, eating avidly and smacking her lips and looking around at the spectators and grinning with the self-satisfaction of little Jack Horner's sister pulling out a plum and saying what a good girl am I.

I learned, however, you can't always regard wild animals as docile household pets. Whenever I pressed Smokey's cold moist black nose with my fore-finger, she automatically opened her mouth for the next treat; it was like power windows in a car. But one evening, when she was already chewing up a dog cookie I gave her, I pressed her nose – and she snapped. I grabbed my fingers back just in time. I was getting too close to her food.

(Years before I had the same experience in Salisbury, New Brunswick – back in the days when many service stations had young bear cubs chained to stakes as tourist attractions. At a time when pop was selling for five cents a bottle, these stations charged motorists five cents also for improvised "bear pop" containing water and less than a cent's worth of sugar. The bear would sit up and glug this right down out of the bottle like an old soak. Feeling sorry for the Salisbury bear, I used to bring him blueberry branches laden with lush berries. I fed the branches slowly into his long mouth. Incredibly, any green berries poured out both sides of his snout as he chewed; he had a natural built-in separator. One day as I stood even closer, feeding the branch in – *wham!* – I found myself sitting down, dazed, on the earth. A passing farmhand said, "He took a swipe at you because you were getting too handy to his eating.")

It was early summer when we suspected Smokey had a family of young raccoons hidden away.

When I fed her on the back lawn, she would suddenly pause, sit up erect and listen over her shoulder. I couldn't hear a thing, but she would leave cherished treats and dart into the hole under the garage.

Of course, raccoons are always warily alert to strange sounds. If a train whistle blows, they vanish. If a neighbour starts a power saw, they're gone. But in this case Smokey was attuned to something beyond my hearing, something very important to her.

For weeks we didn't see any sign of young raccoons.

Then one night we were entertaining some in-laws, and the time went faster than we thought. We snapped on the back light at 2 A.M. and peered out the kitchen window.

There, in the dog's fenced-in run, was Smokey shepherding four gambolling baby raccoons as playful as kittens. They laboriously jumped, climbed and pulled themselves up each step leading to what we call the "dog's room" in the garage (he's in the kitchen at night). They were batting each other off the steps, biting each other, hauling each other down.

We all thought how fortunate we were. We'd probably never see a litter of raccoons again.

A month later, the under-the-garage population increased again. Big booby Cindy, the father, was long since gone, apparently leaving the entire infant-training chore to his mate while he tried his social graces on other females in the woods.

Three new arrivals had moved in – a huge, round, fat male raccoon we immediately called The Godfather; a mother raccoon dubbed Mrs. Kung Fu, who, when she came within a distance of three feet, levelled her paw horizontally at you in the traditional Kung Fu pre-fight stance; and Midge, a tiny raccoon, evidently her daughter, who came closer but struck the same pose.

So now there were evidently two households under the garage. They weren't friendly, but merely tolerated each other; sometimes we heard growls and scrambles and fights and yipes. But we didn't see Smokey and her little ones. Apparently she spent most of her time out in the forest giving them their first woodcraft training.

The Kung Fu family became quite tame. At least, the Godfather did. The others would come fairly near, grab a treat out of your hand as fast as a railway mail-car snatching a bag hanging from a siding; you had to look down to see if you had a scratch. But the Godfather was as gentle as an English sheepdog. When I sat out at night on the concrete step by the back door, flashlight in hand, he'd waddle across the lawn from the garage, then across the limestone driveway, and look at my feet.

If I was wearing pigskin slip-on shoes, he'd put one paw on my left foot, another on my knee, and reach up with both paws for the treat.

But if I was wearing my best black shoes, he'd look down and hesitate as if he didn't want to spoil the shine, and stand up on his hind legs unassisted and put his paw on my knee. Unlike Smokey, he took treats first in his paws and then put them in his mouth. I told myself that even when Smokey's litter grew up, and resemblances perhaps became confused, I could always tell one raccoon from another – if I ever saw them again – by the various ways they accepted treats.

Early one evening – an extraordinary evening – I was trying to cajole the Godfather and Mrs. Kung Fu and Midge into coming out from under the garage.

All of a sudden I heard crashing noises from the woods. And out came Smokey, galloping, leading a parade of four little raccoons, strung out Indian file, their black masks making them all look like juvenile bank-robbers.

The mother rushed over to my feet. I reached down and fed her a biscuit.

Young raccoons take their cue instantly from their mother. When they saw her eating from my hand, they all hugged my ankles in their arms and started chewing on my loafers, because I represented Old Grandfather Food.

Then, to my amazement, Smokey left her family in my care. She ambled back to the hole under the garage, emerged immediately again inside the dog's run where the grass was entirely worn off, and stretched out her tortured nursing stomach on the nice cool moist evening soil, her front legs flat-out ahead and her rear legs extended back of her, watching me with evident parental approval. She was glad to see someone else feeding them for a change.

This sign of approval the young ones never forgot. Whenever I went out to the garage corner and called, "Hi, hi, hi, hi! *Look, look, look, look!*" they all came sprinting out together. They sprinted so fast it reminded me of a free-wheeling Roman chariot race coming at me five-abreast – or a professional football offensive line charging straight at me.

It's a well-known maxim of wild animal feeding that two raccoons come to you twice as fast as one, because neither wants the other to get there first. From my own experience, five come five times as fast.

I always ran.

Around and around the lawn I raced, sometimes dancing backward as I frantically tossed down bits of bread to delay the thundering herd until I could make a break for the back door. It took nimble footwork, because they were faster.

Even when I succeeded in getting into the porch, there was no respite. The little devils lined up standing on the step, banging on the screen door.

Eventually one of them always managed to open the door with his paw, holding it wide and looking at me as if to say, "What's been keeping you?"

I'd taken the precaution of sprinkling the floor of the five-by-five-foot porch with bits of dog biscuit, so they wouldn't grab my ankles when they came storming in. It was a wild melee. They all tried to squeeze in at the same time, creating a traffic jam. I attempted to control things by warding off some with my foot and pushing others with my hand; it was always a surprise to discover how much their fur felt like steel wool.

They didn't seem to mind being shoved. That was another thing I learned. If you handle a raccoon from infancy, you can keep handling it with little fear of wild-animal reaction, because you are sort of a second parent.

Characteristically, they were inquisitive – and acquisitive – beyond belief. One young raccoon ran past me, poked the cellar door open and dashed down the stairs, making a complete circuit of the basement before passing me again on its way upstairs as I hurried down.

By now another raccoon had lifted the cover off the garbage pail in the porch; two were standing up looking into it.

The last young raccoon grabbed a clean dish towel in its mouth and fled out the open back doorway toward the garage, the dish towel streaming out behind.

"Hey you, bring that back!" I shouted, running after it.

I almost got the dish towel, because the raccoon paused for a moment at the hole. But just as I slowed up to bend down and reach for it, the other raccoons caught up and affectionately grabbed me around the ankles.

Desperately I hop-skipped around, trying to extricate myself without falling.

The dish towel disappeared.

Out of sheer necessity, I became quite good at fending off the rampaging family. I discovered that any sudden and unusual noise would put them to rout – once. After the first time they paid no heed. One device I used was to scrape my shoes back and forth on the driveway, like a roaring growl-sound, which required me to do a fast clog-dance.

Several times I saw neighbours looking over in the twilight wondering what I was doing at this time of night. I only hope they thought I was trying to scrape chewing gum off my soles.

Another stratagem I used was either to growl out loud, like a fierce threat, or to blow air out rapidly through my vibrating pursed lips, like a horse going *flubbbbbbbbbbbb!* on a cold winter's day, with clouds of steam rising from its mouth and nostrils. This sent the raccoons flying, and brought the neighbours to the edge of their gardens.

But it was an awful let-down the second time around, when I clog-danced energetically and growled and blew blasts of air through my lips and the raccoons didn't even look up from their eating. They thought I took these spells every so often.

I learned also the best way to get raccoons out of the porch: a broom. You see, they won't leave on request; if you push one out, it'll come back while you're pushing the next one out; no raccoon wants to be out while some are in.

It took some fancy broomwork; if you've ever seen a curler desperately sweeping the ice as if his life depended on it, you'll know what I mean.

It was easy to tumble one raccoon out gently, head over heels; but then you had to bundle at least two more out before it tried to come back, until finally you had them all out and, holding your foot out to block the entrance, got the screen door shut. Meanwhile the tension wasn't lessened much by the fact a German shepherd was sniffing at the crack under the kitchen door, hoping someone would open it by mistake.

Raccoons are quick thinkers. When you sent one of them rolling into the darkness on the outswing of the broom, he'd often embrace it tight with his front and back legs and travel happily back into the porch on the insweep.

But it was worth all the trouble to have wild friends who would come out from under the garage and sit and commune with you on the back step when things at home got upset or company was boring.

Smokey, in fact, became so tame she came out in mid-day

when I knocked on the shingles above her entrance – unusual for a nocturnal animal.

Once I knocked at suppertime, because I had my inexpensive camera all set up and the sunlight was good. Several visitors were watching.

Out came Smokey. I was on my knees to get a closeup shot. Seeing the camera held in front of my face, she stood up on her hind legs and came slowly waddling over to me as I snapped pictures. Then she took the camera in her two paws, on the opposite side from me, and began chewing on it – if I was offering something in her direction, it naturally must be good to eat.

She had a marvellous sense of smell. One summer midafternoon my wife came in from back of the house, where she had been resting on a lounge-chair with a basket of biscuits on a lawn table beside her. I looked out the kitchen window and there was Smokey, standing up and reaching in and filching biscuits out of the basket. When she had difficulty getting them all, she climbed up on top of the lounge chair to do it better. By this time I was out taking progressive pictures of the heist; but Smokey continued, unperturbed, because I was only another raccoon.

Smokey didn't seem to be afraid of strangers as long as they were with me. One evening we had a Jesuit seminarian as a guest. A former housekeeper also visiting us had a bright orange VW "Thing" parked at the back door, and as this style of car was new in our area, I said to the priest: "Come out with me and I'll show you something pretty unusual."

He followed me out, but didn't even notice The Thing – because out of the darkness around the corner came an erect raccoon walking to meet him, her hands held out to the sides appealingly.

"Great heavens!" he exclaimed when we came in. "That *was* something else!"

Gradually, we saw less and less of Smokey. We heard of a

large raccoon leading a procession of smaller raccoons across a lawn half a mile away, and sheltering under a house there. But about once a month they'd come rollicking back, ravenous for hand-outs, and difficult to distinguish from one another now because the young ones looked as big as their mother.

I worried a lot about Smokey's family when they were with us, because people disagree sharply about whether raccoons are cute lovable creatures or diabolical children of Satan himself.

Some visitors say: "Oh, I'd *adore* to see them – I think raccoons are just the sweetest."

Others: "Don't tell me you're feeding *raccoons!*" – uttering the last word in extreme horror, as if you've been caught cultivating bacteriological warfare germs in your bathtub.

And the neighbours didn't exactly throw their hats in the air when they heard I was playing landlord to two raccoon families.

One man, who had a large vegetable garden, told me in the fall: "The raccoons got into my corn last night." He kindly refrained from saying "your" raccoons, but he added, "They can strip a corn field in one night, you know." I was afraid he planned to shoot them, but he said he was going to put out a defence line of moth balls, which someone suggested was a sure preventative.

I can imagine. The resourceful raccoons probably carried them back to their home and used them to keep moths out of their stolen woollens.

Another neighbour said little, but came by in the late fall wearing a large raccoon hat. "Made it myself a few years back," he said. "Whenever I spy one I plug it quick."

So you can see why I worried when Smokey started taking her youngsters around on educational excursions.

When my wife and I left for a month's trip to the west coast, we tried to impress on our younger son and his wife, who were looking after the house, that some day the "motor-cycle gang," as we called Smokey's lusty brood, might descend on them.

We heard about it when we were in Edmonton, Alberta. My son was outdoors in the evening, trying to coax the shy Kung Fu family out from under the garage, when a tumult came from the woods and out charged a line of raccoons – the motorcycle gang. They climbed right up his legs and torso, each jumping to haul the others down.

I was glad to think, when we returned in December, that all the raccoons would soon be hibernating for the cold months – a blessed surcease for everyone.

I decided that after this they could go their own way and look after themselves, because I was only making welfare bums out of them. If they caused trouble in the neighbour-hood, they'd have to take the consequences. I would never stand up for them again. I'd had it.

Just then another neighbour dropped in and said meaning-fully, "The raccoons got into my cellar one night when you were away. They also honked my car horn at three o'clock in the morning and woke us all up."

Well, of course! I don't know what he expected if he was so careless as to leave his cellar unlocked and his car window open. Naturally a raccoon, being a raccoon, would want to see what happened if you pressed that soft padded leather in the centre of the steering wheel, because how else would he ever find out?

That man was just lucky they didn't turn the ignition key and drive his stupid car across the main road into the Kennebecasis River.

65

The Macaw,
the Lady and I

When a woman standing in a crowd of people yells, "Shut your mouth!" at her husband, you'd think he'd be pretty annoyed at her.

I wasn't put out at all when it happened to me. In fact, I thanked her. It shows what a remarkably forbearing husband I must be.

To begin at the beginning –

It's captivating to see what they've taught macaws and cockatoos and other exotic species to do in the noon-hour bird show at Busch Gardens in Tampa, Florida.

Those cockatoos especially with their luxuriant feathered head-dresses – almost North American Indian style – enthrall the kids.

They glide down chutes, salute Old Glory, haul fire engines to answer emergency alarms, pull the strings to fire off cannons, rescue the princess from the mediaeval castle where the evil ogre has been holding her prisoner.

Afterward the trainer announces that people wishing to take snapshots of their friends holding macaws on their arms may do so by following a path to a secluded spot a few yards away, where attendants will assist them.

The radiantly plumed macaws, of course, were designed by nature for colour photo fans. They sit quietly when placed on your extended arm, and give any snapshot authentic tropical atmosphere.

There is, however, one minor hazard.

"Please be sure," the attendants kept repeating to us, "you are not wearing any bright jewellery like earrings or necklaces that might attract the birds' attention, or they will try to take them."

All the way down the line-up of waiting patrons, women began removing glittering bracelets and pins and other silver and gold and gemstone ornaments.

Just as I was about to reach the head of the line, a fat, mascara-painted woman in slacks rushed up and vigorously elbowed in ahead of me.

"I came here before," she rasped. "I had to go look for my old man; so I'm still first."

Without another word she pushed me back, hurried up to the attendant and held out her arms to demand the macaws.

I noticed – I couldn't say exactly with horror – she was wearing a very fine gold-coloured necklace.

It happened in the blink of an eye. The first macaw on her arm looked, raised its head suddenly to see even more clearly. And then with lightning thrusts of its curved beak – so fast the human eye could scarcely follow – the bird went *snip-snip-snip-snip!* and the necklace disappeared in a dozen tiny driblets into the sand underfoot.

The woman, aghast, was left holding her bare neck as if she was suddenly naked.

The onlookers guffawed.

My turn was next. I now felt for some reason elated, even frolicsome.

The attendants put a brilliant red, blue, green and gold macaw on each of my arms. My wife hurriedly adjusted the lens on our camera.

To assume what I thought was a comic pose, I held one arm up higher and opened my mouth with the macaw looking in as if it were a dentist. I shut my eyes.

They tell me the macaw stared for a fascinated moment, quickly raised its head to get a clearer view, and –

"Shut your mouth!" my wife yelled.

I wheeled around then glared at her in a mixture of amazement, disbelief and embarrassment. Then the realization struck me: I have a prominent gold eye-tooth on what my childhood dentist always called "the lower floor."

There's no doubt that the macaw, with his unerring aim and stunning striking power, would have extracted the gold cap in a twinkling.

How could I have faced my dentist when I returned to Canada?

It was bad enough to try to tell him about it as a bit of casual chair-talk while he mixed plastic cement in a little jar.

I said, "I almost lost that gold tooth while I was in Florida."

"Oh? How?" Now he was holding two drill-points up to the light.

"Well, there was this bird like a big parrot –"

"Did you bite on it?" – incredulously.

"No, no; you see, it was looking in my mouth –"

"Why?"

"Well, you see, it was sort of a tableau – what I mean, the bird was sort of acting the role of the dentist."

"Yes, I see perfectly" – but his expression looked baffled.

"I thought it would make an unusual photo," I explained.

"I'm sure it would."

That's the trouble with dentists these days. They get so engrossed in their professional work they can't even follow an ordinary conversation.

Goodbye,
Chippy Chipmunk

When we summered at Epworth Park, I told bedtime stories about the adventures of Chippy Chipmunk to our first son, then a small boy.

Chippy was a recklessly venturesome youngster who sometimes paid little attention to what his mother said. One day he left the shelter of the big log they lived in, against her advice, and started out to explore the open meadow.

Down dived a hungry hawk and scooped up Chippy in its sharp talons, carrying him high into the sky.

Daddy Chipmunk heard the faint cries of "Help! Help!" and realized immediately what had happened.

Luckily he knew a man in the suburban resort who had a discarded Second World War fighter plane. Daddy Chipmunk jumped into it, took off with a roar, soon saw the hawk and zoomed up behind it. He fired a burst from his guns so accurately that half the hawk's feathers flew off, and the big bird began to flounder and sink.

One more *rackety-rack-rack* from the machine guns and the hawk let go of Chippy and crashed down on the ground. Chippy plummeted down into a tall white birch tree that cushioned his fall.

The little chipmunk was quickly reunited with his family back in the log. It was a great celebration, because this happened to be his first birthday and his mother had baked and frosted a lovely hazelnut cake with one blue candle burning on it. Chippy promised never again to go out into the field until his parents said he could.

Well, maybe the story was a little on the fantastic side.

But there *was* a real-life Chippy Chipmunk.

He, too, went through hair-raising experiences, if somewhat different.

Our first summer in Epworth Park we spent in a small cottage on a corner lot between the steep incoming road and a crossroad. Occasional trucks rumbling along the crossroad made the thin walls tremble.

To get to the lawn in front of the cottage, you walked down three old stone steps.

Right away we noticed a chipmunk had a home under a corner of the lowest step. He would emerge from the hole, jump up the steps, scamper along a log beside the crossroad to our verandah.

One day, when we were having lunch just inside the living-room with the front door open, we heard a pattering on the verandah. The chipmunk, moving in erratic spurts like a First World War movie, looked in.

We kept still; he didn't stay long. But in a day or two he sallied into the front room itself, remained a few seconds, and quick-footed away.

Every day he got bolder. We'd hear the pittery-pitter of paw-steps, then he'd come in and sit up like a pet dog, waiting for someone to throw him a treat.

Finally he reached up with both paws – or even jumped up like an outfielder snagging a line drive – to take food out of your hand.

He never swallowed. Always he put the morsel into one of his cheeks, and he never left until he had both cheeks completely full and he looked as though he had an acute case of mumps.

Away he'd go, trippety-tripping along the verandah floor and then along the log, down the stone steps and into the hole.

Chippy Chipmunk, as we named him, became a daily guest at the table, or below it. He seemed to know the exact time we were going to eat; the ice man, the milk man, the bread man might.fail to show up, but never Chippy. We looked forward to his visits – the entire average of ten visits every meal.

We marvelled, too, to think what a luxuriant stock of groceries he must be hoarding away in his subterranean warehouse for the winter – far more, proportionate to his size, than a human could jam into a basement of deep-freezes. We imagined walk-in rows labelled "Nuts," "Crusts," "Crackers" and "Candy."

But Chippy had one very bad habit. He was too trusting. He acted as if he had never heard of cats or traffic hazards.

Every afternoon he sat up erect on top of the long log – a handsome chipmunk with black and white stripes down his tawny back – watching the cars and trucks go by. They held endless fascination for him. It reminded me of stories I'd heard about Mounties returning from three years of solitude in the Canadian Arctic and sitting for hours on the Sparks Street curb in Ottawa, unable to wrench their eyes away from the astounding spectacle of cars whizzing past.

Actually, Chippy looked more like a spectator at a Wimbledon tennis final; his head kept swivelling left, right, left, right.

We were naturally anxious for Chippy's safety, because he was a sitting duck for any predator. But when nothing happened for two months, we decided Chippy was protected by his own special lucky star.

Then it happened.

One suppertime as the family was sitting down to the table, I looked out the front window. There looking back at me from the lawn was the Rhodes' beautiful orange Persian cat.

Hanging limp and silent from its mouth was Chippy, his head and front paws drooping from one side, the back paws and tail from the other.

I'm embarrassed now to say how I reacted.

With a bellowing roar I leaped up from the table, vaulted over the verandah railing and, shouting at the top of my lungs, chased the cat headlong through the dense woods leading to a low cliff over the St. John River a hundred yards away.

Before I knew it, I'd reached the cliff. No cat. Somewhere along the way it had swerved left or right. I could never save Chippy now, even if by any chance he had survived that first awful bite into his back.

It would be hard to say how deeply dejected our household was in the days that followed. No one talked about the chipmunk. No one had much appetite. I've had many close human friends whose death didn't evoke such a personal depth of grief. Most pet owners have experienced this and have felt vaguely guilty about it and wondered why it was. The reason probably is that humans can talk and understand the risks ahead. Pet animals can't talk and understand; they only have implicit loving faith – as their eyes show – that you will always be good to them – and they still look up at you the same way in decrepit old age when you are deliberately taking them to the vet's to be given the lethal 14-gauge needle. That's what tears the heart out of their owners.

Chippy had not been quite that personal a pet, but he did trust us, and we felt terrible. We only wished there had been some way to warn him of the perils of sitting out in public by the hour with cats around.

(Even so, we learned later that in the normal course of events Chippy might not have become a casualty. The Rhodes had gone away for a week and left their teen-age son

Charlie in charge at home. Charlie had completely forgotten to feed the cat. So the big orange Persian set forth to forage for itself.)

A week went by, with no lightening of the pall of grief and remorse at home.

Then, one noon-time, we had just sat down when we heard a strange noise on the verandah – a grating, shuffling sound.

We all looked to the doorway.

To our astonishment, there was Chippy Chipmunk!

He was hauling his body along with his front paws, his hind legs dragging. Down the length of his back was an ugly irregular purple scar, half healed.

The cat, terrified, had dropped him and fled.

Laboriously he came in. We fed him. He was starved. He didn't fill his cheeks – he ate.

After he dragged himself out again, we wondered whether we'd have a hopelessly crippled pet. It might have been better if Chippy had been killed outright.

But each day he returned, and each day he became visibly nimbler. He regained the use of his hind legs, and the long scar began to fade.

Within two more weeks Chippy was practically his old self again, skittering along the verandah and coming in to sit up expectantly.

In September we had misgivings about moving back to the city. Who'd feed Chippy? Then we realized he had a super-market full of foodstuffs stashed away. We ourselves should be half as lucky.

A month and a half later, as November's chill was beginning to grip the land, we made a special trip back to Epworth Park just to see. The summer colony was strangely vacant; every sound, even a crunching footstep on the gravel path, echoed loudly in the ghostly silence.

Suddenly, out of nowhere, Chippy appeared, sprinting up to our feet, looking up at a bag in my hands and leaping up high and nudging it. I'd almost forgotten about the peanuts for him.

He was never tamer, never happier to see us. He kept jumping and holding up his paws. Apparently he thought we'd all be delighted to stand in the deserted side-road each time while he ran back to his underground home to unload.

We returned to the park once more, in mid-December, when the first snows had fallen.

No sign of Chippy anywhere.

We finally walked down the stone steps, intending to call him out of the hole underneath.

But it was tightly plugged with a small apple.

He had gone in for the winter and closed the door.

Whatever Became
of Doris Duck?

It was a great feeling: I had a wild duck for a pet! By a stroke of good fortune I had acquired what surely was the most inexpensive pet in the entire world.

You see, Doris – that was her name – could forage for her own food in the Intracoastal Waterway behind our condominium at Indian Shores, Florida, which fronted on the Gulf of Mexico.

She could sleep, as she unquestionably preferred, on the sand flats under the boardwalk joining the T-shaped boat piers.

In short, I'd have no expense whatever except a few daily treats, which might be merely left-overs from the dinner table. (This matter of expense, as any pet owner knows, can be a serious affair. Many an old lady recluse today spends twelve dollars a week on her dog, in addition to five dollars a week on groceries for herself, to make sure her pet gets all the proteins, minerals, vitamins and the other things that Madison Avenue assures us are essential to animal health – necessities that my mother never knew about while somehow managing, in sheer ignorance, to bring up six surprisingly healthy dogs in turn as well as seven healthy children.)

Ironically, the first twenty times I saw Doris, all I caught a glimmer of was her backside – a bobbing white turned-up tail disappearing around the timber piles under one of the piers. She was always elusive, a will-o'-the-wisp.

Somebody who knew ducks said it was a female mallard – he could tell from her brown feathers with beautiful iridescent glints of green and blue.

To everyone's surprise, including my own, I tamed Doris with beer pretzels.

A travelling vendor had come to the condominium with a vanload of giant potato chips, popcorn, corn puffs, also several sizes of pretzels. For a joke I had bought the biggest, which looked almost like starved doughnuts twisting in anguish. As no one ate them, I took several down to the waterfront, crumbled them and tossed the bits out in the duck's direction.

Doris loved them. Day by day she became more trusting; she swam closer and closer to where I stood on the pier. Her bill darted this way and that as she ate voraciously, making a happy squidgey-squishing talk that sounded partly like chewing in water, partly like contented purring in a low quacking voice. Then she would cock her head and look up at me with one eye to see if I was throwing out some more.

It wasn't until one day when Doris, cruising around, made her wings go like airplane propellers revving up while she stood upright momentarily in the water, shaking the wet out of them, that I saw they were clipped. She had evidently grown up in a commercial tourist show-place, and escaped. But as she couldn't join her wild cousins on their annual migration northward to Canada, she was reluctantly willing to be a friend to anyone who she was sure was offering friendship.

But I should explain how Doris got her name. In our

condominium there was a genial grandmother from Ohio whose first name was Doris. She often walked down to the pier to look on as the duck swam around so effortlessly.

"I never learned to swim," she confessed, adding with a sigh, "When I go into the pool I just pretend and make my arms go."

Watching Doris slurp-eating bits of pretzel, she said, "I've always thought that I'd like to come back as a duck in my next reincarnation."

A long silence ensued. Then she mused: "If you're ever feeding pretzels to a duck some day, and after you get through she still keeps looking up at you, lower a can of beer – it's me!"

My newly named duck became so tame she would jump out of a wave and land right on the pier, and walk around. Soon she preferred to snooze only on the pier in the daytime, with her head turned around backwards and her bill buried in her feathers.

The remarkable thing was how good everyone was to Doris. You'd think some clod would get the idea this was a golden chance to bring home a duck dinner, and simply crack her over the head with a baseball bat. But even the roughest-hewn characters – professional fishermen who set down huge box traps for blue-claw crabs – were thoughtful enough to bring a bag of old bread to feed to Doris, although sometimes they looked around first as if fearful of being mistaken for softies.

Several fascinated people in the condominium began to feed her, too, and watched cluckingly as Doris performed quackingly. In her loneliness she palled around with an old greying seagull. They would swim together to the embankment under the boardwalk where a fresh-water pipe emptied into the waterway and, like two kids, would open their bills, tilt their heads back and let the drip pour in.

Most of the time Doris hated seagulls, because they had a

habit of swooping down out of nowhere and grabbing off some of her treats from the waves just as she was getting ready to sluice them through her bill. Even if infuriated, Doris had too much sense to attack her bigger tormentors. Instead, she hissed at them. Unfortunately she didn't have a good hiss like a goose. She went through the motions, but it sounded as if she was just exhaling her breath at them.

Out in the 400-yard-wide waterway, she sometimes socialized with several strange white-and-black ducks; as mallards rarely came around, any ducks were better than none. But most of the time she stayed in close to the protective overhang of the two piers and the boardwalk connecting them, and avoided the open water. A sudden dark shadow overhead seemed to frighten her – a fear perhaps originating in infancy when predatory birds like hawks sometimes flashed down on the scattering ducklings. Even at her tamest, I noticed, if I was flicking down pieces of pretzel and I made an unexpected quick move above her, Doris vanished beneath the boardwalk in a showering flurry of wings and webbed feet. It may have been, too, that with her wings clipped she couldn't easily duck down and swim under the surface when danger hovered.

It was all a very idyllic master-and-pet relationship. There were, in fact, only one or two slight drawbacks.

Doris eventually decided that as I owned her, or she owned me – I never got it clear – she wanted her rights.

She became assertive and demanding.

At 6.45 A.M. every day I was catapulted out of bed in a tangle of arms and legs when I heard the call from the waterway, as loud as an old-fashioned Klaxon horn in staccato tempo:

WACK WACK WACK WACK WACK *Wack Wack Wack Wack Wack Wack . . .!*

She was saying, "Come and feed me!"

I grabbed a plastic bag of old bread as I rushed past the

kitchen, because I didn't want her to wake up the other 123 families in the condominium, which might arouse public opinion to get rid of her. I learned not to squander valuable seconds hauling up my pants and buttoning a shirt. It was 50 per cent faster to cast off my pajama top (all I wore) and jump into a pair of swim trunks, as if I were going to the pool, then slam my feet into a pair of slippers on the run and dash down the hallway donning a terrycloth beach coat.

Yet somehow I couldn't be angry at Doris; I always found her swimming around in aimless circles, waiting for me. And did she ever relish those first pretzel and bread bits to start the day off full of energy!

But the problem didn't stop there. When I walked down to the swimming pool and out to the boardwalk, even among fifty other men and women, I heard:

WACK! . . . WACK! . . . WACK! . . . WACK! . . . WACK! (meaning "Wait! . . . Wait! . . . Wait! . . . Wait!") And I'd look down the waterway to see a duck an eighth of a mile away making its wings go like propellers again and running on top of the water like a biblical miracle.

This spectacle caused what writers of the 1890's would have called much good-natured merriment. People marvelled at how Doris could always spot me. Some said ducks had extraordinary eyesight. Others averred it was her acute sense of smell, which, at an eighth of a mile away, didn't make me any happier. Nor did my wife's theory – that Doris knew me by my walk, which, she insisted, was remarkably like a duck's.

This caused me to study my reflection in the plateglass doors of the condominium every time I came up to them in a swimsuit. Was that man walking normally? Or was there just a touch of middle-age bandy-leggedness, like the testy British colonial governor of Bermuda in a costume movie? Sometimes, just to get the comparison, I deliberately waddled. This upset my wife, but, as I reminded her, I wouldn't have

tried to walk like a duck if she hadn't brought up the sugges-
tion.

If I went now to a party on the top floor of the condominium, and wandered out to the patio with some guests
and carried on a normal conversation, it was only moments
before I heard:

WAAAAK! WAAAAAK! WAAAAAK!

– and, looking far down, I could see a tiny speck swimming
around and around with its head tilted to one side, looking
up. She had heard me. Many a guest must have wondered
why I abruptly dashed out of the party. Did I have intestinal
flu? Was I mad about something? If so, why did I grab up a
handful of cocktail crackers and wrap them in a napkin? Did
crackers cool off my heated emotions?

I was hurrying, of course, to mollify Doris. Once she had
eaten her fill, she'd let me be until the next morning.

But that wasn't her most exasperating habit. As time went
on, she became bolder. When I appeared on the boardwalk,
she'd race over to the pier, hop up on it, run pell-mell along
the cross-walk and then down the long wooden pier to me so
fast I always thought she would pitch forward flat on her
face. Then she ravenously ate up all the treats I placed
around the boards.

The trouble now was, she wanted to come with me after
she ate. I'd say, "Goodbye, Doris," and start to walk away
toward the swimming pool – and everyone would burst out
laughing. When I turned around, she was right behind me,
walking in my footsteps like a child showing off, and – awful
thought – waddling just like me.

I scolded Doris, pointed my finger at her reproachfully
and, with my hands shoving her gently, walked her all the
way back to the boardwalk while she protested in loud
squidgey talk, looking at me first over her left shoulder and
then over her right, as if I was treating her very inconsider-
ately.

"Now," I said, "go into the water! Go where you belong! I'll see you tomorrow."

I turned and walked away – a roar of laughter exploded again. She hadn't listened to one word; she was marching along in my footsteps again, as blithe as ever.

As I knew there would be irate rumblings from some of the other residents if she came near the swimming pool, I had no choice but to stay down on the pier with Doris. This delighted her; she ambled around and quack-talked animatedly about important things – the weather, the seagulls and the pretzel crop, as far as I could tell – and finally went to sleep on the boardwalk, with her feathers bedded down and her head on backwards.

Several people began to wonder what had happened between my wife and myself; we never sat together any more.

I gradually began to discern I was not the owner of a duck; I was the slave of a duck.

I didn't dare go away for a day without making arrangements for someone to be a duck-sitter – to get up early and feed Doris, and listen for her through the day.

I began imagining with a start, when I was strolling through a shopping mall and heard a stereo shop playing a quack-quack-quack bassoon interlude in blatty guttural notes, I could hear Doris calling, and involuntarily reached in my pocket for the bag of treats. The place was lucky I wasn't really absent-minded. I might have scattered pretzel bits all over the music-room floor.

But the worst extreme came when I realized Doris was actually causing me physical pain. My nose was blistering red in the southern sun. I tried lotions; it seemed to get redder.

A helpful friend bought me a twenty-nine-cent white plastic nose-guard in the drug store, the kind you fasten on to your glasses. It was just what I needed!

When I walked down to the swimming pool, the reaction from the sun-bathers was immediate and enthusiastic.

"Here he comes, Daddy Duck! Quack, quack, quack, quack!"

"They'll all follow you now; where are your tail feathers?"

"There's an egret looking at you. You've got the skinny legs – why don't you wear a longer bill?"

I didn't wear my artificial beak any more; I just got more blisters.

A week before we left The Bay Mariner to return to Canada, Doris unaccountably disappeared. There was not even a pin-feather to be seen. Endlessly I trod up and down the lonely piers, scanning the sand flats, looking with growing suspicion on every hawk-like bird in the sky, every dog walking by a half-mile away, every hiker who looked hungry.

Never before had I appreciated how good-hearted my neighbours in the condominium were. Minnesota millionaires, New Jersey legislators and Canadian judges patiently walked the waterfront, too, peering everywhere – not so much out of sympathy for Doris, I learned through second-hand conversation, as out of sympathy for me. Poor Mr. Trueman had lost his duck, and nobody could feel right until it was found.

Two days later she re-appeared just as unaccountably, ravenous and as affectionate as ever.

Then she vanished again. She came back in two days, but promptly evaporated for a third time.

The morning we left for Canada, she was still away. It was a sad day. Yet it was a relief, too. Perhaps (happy thought) she had other interests, and wouldn't be on my mind and conscience any more.

Dutifully I dropped a big supply of pretzel bits between the planks of the boardwalk down to the sand flats.

Often in the months that followed we talked about Doris. We thought of all the duck language we had learned – "It's time to feed me!," "Wait up!," "Boy, these pretzels are good!," "Come down off that patio," and, when she was making her way from one lounge-chair to another among the sun-tanners, a soft-spoken "Duk-duk-duk?," meaning, "Got anything to eat?"

We had one tangible, visible souvenir: the movie interlude that my wife made of the two of us walking along the pier. It always made her laugh; I still can't see why.

In mid-summer we got a letter from Florida: Doris had returned yet once again, but had vanished forever two weeks after we departed.

When we drove down south the next winter, Doris was still gone. Our friends among the permanent residents mentioned it to us in hushed voices. One woman, after consulting a vet to ascertain the best food, had even bought a sack of corn, but after waiting for weeks, finally had to throw it out. A man was certain Doris must have ended up on somebody's dinner table. Another woman thought that the duck perhaps had got hurt or become ill, and I should look around at the Suncoast Seabird Sanctuary only a mile down Gulf Boulevard.

Then a gruff and abrupt-talking fishermen's outfitter nearby, a Mr. Mahuffer, told me: "I was there, myself, so I should know. This handsome drake, with lots of brilliant colour in his feathers – he came struttin' around the pier in front of Doris last May. I saw him, oh, several times. And one day Doris swam away with him."

I don't listen to any more versions now, because I like that one best.

The Strangers Under
the Garage Floor

It was a wonderful way of entertaining guests, while it lasted.

You see, in Rothesay on the Kennebecasis River, we have a very distinctive garage. If garages were collectible like antiques, this one would be worth more than a brand-new house. The peak-roofed building, shingled and painted, looks outwardly modern, but actually it's venerable – nearly a century old.

Of course, at that age, it wasn't built for automobiles. It was a deluxe barn – a carriage house and horse stable. The heavy-timbered stall is still there, a manger at the rear, and beside it a wooden window-door part-way up the end wall.

(I was going to say "a window-door to fork the hay in," but my wife, who comes from the country, corrects me: "That was to shovel the horse manure out. The hay was forked down through the opening from the second floor, the loft, after it was pitched in from a wagon through the doors on the end wall of the loft." The point doesn't really matter, I suppose, unless you happened to be someone standing near the window-door and expecting hay to come through it.)

But what makes the garage a genuine heirloom is the fact it has two rooms along the end nearest the house. The larger room we call the "dog's room," because that is where our

German shepherd sleeps on his mat in cold or rainy weather. His wire-fenced run adjoins the end wall. Between the bottom of the garage and the ground there is some open space – as much as nine inches in places – big enough for raccoons but too small for a large dog to squeeze through. So the raccoons raise their families inside in perfect safety – as long as the young ones mind their mother's warnings.

The tiny back room is an old rustic toilet, a two-holer. This enables us, even though we are only a one-car family, to say we have bathroom accommodations for four (including the two bathrooms in the house). There's no need to tell people that one bathroom accommodates two patrons side by side like co-pilots. The important thing is to be able to make an affluent claim offhand without fear of successful contradiction.

Nor is there any need to mention that our seven raccoons, which live under the garage, often come up through the two holes – which I imagine gave old-timers quite a surprise, and would probably even give today's blasé generation a lift, too.

Oh, there's one thing I completely forgot to mention: Our wonderful garage doesn't hold a car. It hasn't been able to for years. That's its only drawback. As North American home owners know, standard cars kept getting longer, but old garages didn't. So we keep our picnic tables, chairs and garden hose in the garage, and we keep our car outside.

Early one spring evening years ago, I strolled out to the garage, slid the wide wooden door open on its rollers, and went in to look for the grass rake.

To my startlement, an agitated cheeping, chirping and whirring came up through the heavy floor planks, the whirring sounding something like pigeons or doves cooing.

I stopped, and the noise stopped.

I said out loud, "Hi! How are you down there?"

Immediately the chirping chorus rose up from under the floor again.

Every time I spoke or walked about, the chirpings went on for several seconds.

At first I thought it was a bird's nest or a bat colony. Then I figured a litter of baby raccoons mistook my footsteps and my voice for their mother.

But what was really astonishing was the public interest the mystery aroused. Strangers began dropping in at the house, asking if they could hear the ghost voices. People I never met before stopped me on the street in Saint John to give me their opinions.

A naturalist felt sure they were skunks.

"Can you smell a skunk odour?" he asked.

"No. Nothing at all."

"Well, now, that could be significant! Skunks don't smell up their own home."

I nodded, even if somehow I didn't get it.

An army colonel phoned from thirty miles away to inform me that without question they were raccoons.

"We've had batches of them over the years," he said. "And the young ones sound exactly like that."

One afternoon a senior lawyer, a Queen's Counsel whom I hardly knew, accosted me on the sidewalk.

Looking around over both shoulders, he said quietly, "I have a personal matter to discuss with you."

My spirits fell. I thought he was going to serve me with a summons.

He leaned forward confidentially, and said in a low voice: "They're groundhogs."

"Groundhogs?"–in surprise. "Where?"

"Under your garage. Have you ever seen one around?"

"No, not in recent years."

"That could be a clue! If you have them, you usually don't see them."

I nodded, but somehow I couldn't get this either.

People passing by were staring. They could tell we were

discussing a Supreme Court case. By the reputation of the lawyer, the suit was worth well over $200,000.

"Several years ago," I admitted, "there was a groundhog sitting up on our back lawn. The dog ran around and around it in circles, like an Indian attack on a covered wagon, but the groundhog kept turning around to face him. Then it made a bolt for some huge exposed tree roots and disappeared. When he chattered his teeth defiantly, it sounded like a machine-gun."

"Well, there you are," the lawyer said, wrapping up the case. "It's groundhogs."

As you can appreciate, what I enjoyed most was taking people out to the garage without telling them what to expect. I would lead them out to the building, motion with my hand for silence, and, looking down at the floor, say loudly:

"Hal-*loooo!* What are you doing down there?"

The visitors always looked at me, then at each other.

A suspenseful momentary silence – then the joyous *"Cheep! Cheep! Whirr! Whirr!"*

One dark night, later than usual, I carried a flashlight as I led our wondering guests out to the garage.

I went through the usual performance.

"Hal-*loooo!* How are you down there?"

Up came a mighty explosion.

PSSSFT – SPAT-BAM!

We fled out pell-mell, dazed, wondering what happened, the blast still echoing in our ears.

It was a few moments before we realized that the mother must have been with the brood. What we heard was a combined growl, spit and roar.

But I'll never forget the very last time.

My bank manager came to call. I was trying to be especially nice to him because I was going to approach him soon about a loan. I could hardly wait to invite him to walk out to the garage with me "if you want to see something peculiar."

He followed me into the garage, and I held up a forefinger for silence. Then I leaned forward and looked in front of my toes.

"Hal-*loooo!* What are you doing down there?"

Silence.

I said more loudly:

"Hal-*loooo!* What are you doing down there?"

Again, silence.

The banker asked, "Is there supposed to be a device down there that answers, 'Shoveling coal'?"

"Just a moment. Hal-*loooo!* How's the weather down there?"

Nothing.

The banker looked at me coldly.

"Are you trying to throw your voice?"

"Just one more second." I jocularly raised my voice. "How's the wheat crop, boys?"

In the loud silence that followed, I began to feel embarrassed.

"Do you know what I think?" I said.

"I can't possibly imagine."

"I think they're gone."

"Who?"

"I don't know. But I'll miss them."

"If you don't know them, how can you miss them?"

"They always talked to me."

He looked at me the same way as before, rather strangely. I've noticed he still looks at me that way, even after all these years. I've never asked him for the loan. As it happened, I went to another bank, only for the reason that it is handier.

We never found out for certain who our under-the-floor guests were. But a week or two after my episode with the banker, when silence was still reigning for the first time in months, my younger son took our dog for a walk in the woods behind our house. Within minutes he came sprinting down the hill, shouting.

"Dad! Come quick! I want to show you something."

I accompanied him back, puffing. It was my turn to wonder what to expect.

"In this clearing!" Mac said. He pointed up.

Six young raccoons were clinging to little tree trunks like telephone linesmen, even to the leaning-back pose.

They were only seven feet off the ground, looking down placidly on us as if bows and arrows had not been invented, let alone rifles.

Our German shepherd, Karl, straining his neck to look up and see them all, didn't even bark.

And no wonder. They'd probably grown up only three or four feet from him. He was their next-door good neighbour.

Do the Birds
Really Know?

When the limp and exhausted heron with the fractured wing was carried into the Suncoast Seabird Sanctuary near St. Petersburg, a course of treatment got under way that was to take weeks. It began with splinting and taping the wing, antibiotic injections, and release of the patient into the reassuring dark silence of a recovery chamber to lessen the danger of shock.

Because this heron happened to look just like another at the sanctuary, they stuck a tiny identifying piece of adhesive tape on a primary feather.

The beautiful long-legged bird slowly regained his strength, flapping both wings and finding them good. And one morning he soared up out of the wire-fenced heron compound and rose gracefully over the palm trees.

"It's always a thrill to see a bird fly away again under its own power," muses youthful Ralph Heath, founder and president of the sanctuary. He adds seriously, and somehow you know he means it, "I'd rather tend a sick pelican or heron than unwrap my Christmas presents."

This case had a strange sequel.

Weeks later, Ralph Heath was checking the heron enclosure when he heard a *tap-tap-tap* on the gate. He swung it open – and in stumbled the former heron patient, with a bit of tape still clinging to a feather, and fell down.

"He had got sick," explained the Bird Man of St. Petersburg, "and he may have known where to come for help. He certainly seemed grateful when we took him in a second time."

Not that it's unusual for former feathered patients to drop in occasionally at the exact feeding hour for a free meal, and even bring friends they owe a party to. They're shrewd about food. But sometimes, too, they arrive back when they are ill or hurt again. Is it mere coincidence? Or do they possess enough intelligence to seek aid in distress?

A visit to the Suncoast Seabird Sanctuary is one of the cheapest – and most moving – tourist experiences in Florida.

It's cheap because it doesn't cost a $3.75 admission fee like some commercial attractions. It doesn't cost a cent. There's a wooden box on a post with a slot you can put a coin in. The money helps buy food for the patients.

It's moving not only because of the pitiful birds – 90 per cent of them injured by man – that the sanctuary successfully restores to health, and because of the good care received by the cripples that have become permanent inmates, but also because so many poor parents mingle with the middle-class and rich who bring their youngsters to see the more than 700 patients.

"We can't afford to go anywhere else," one father tells me, simply. He drops in a quarter. It helps.

Driving down the Gulf of Mexico shore toward St. Petersburg, amid so many Bide-a-Wee beach cottage signs, you may easily miss the cut-out pelican signpost between motels that invites the passerby to turn in to the sanctuary grounds.

The place seems slightly exotic at first glance. Many of the birds' runs are so thickly roofed over with long-leafed thatching you may think you've inadvertently wandered into a Polynesian island.

"Hi!" says a raspy but cheerful voice back of us, like a teen-ager with a cold. "HI! HI! HI!"

I swing around. It's a black fish-crow looking at me with button eyes. His beak is protruding through the wire mesh of his big cage, silently waiting for me to offer a treat, though he has plenty of bird food on his floor. He wants to try whatever's going.

Two other crows share his cage. A sign says they are Icha-bod, Eddie and Vladimir and they know several words.

The beak quickly grasps a piece of bread I hold out, then drops it disdainfully to the cage floor.

As I turn away, a phone rings in the distance, and a croaky voice behind me yells helpfully, "TELEPHONE!"

All around are cages, thatched-over runs and open compounds where tall egrets, huge-jowled pelicans, baleful turkey vultures and fifty other species waddle or stalk about – birds with names as intriguing as black-bellied plover, red-bellied woodpecker and red-breasted merganser, knot, anthinga or snake bird, lesser and greater scaup, oyster catcher, laughing gull and mourning dove, helmet pigeon, Chuck Wills widow, sandwich tern, clapper rail.

Some of the names evoke a picture of a feathered United Nations – Muscovy duck, Peking duck, Egyptian goose, Chinese goose, European goose, Canada goose, American scooter, Florida gallinule.

Immediately you notice the patients are wearing red, blue or yellow plastic legbands.

"Red means they're recovering and will be returned to the wild, perhaps soon," explains a passing volunteer youth. "Blue means they're still under observation. Yellow, they're here for life – about 75 per cent of the birds you see."

Sure enough, most of the yellow-banded pelicans are hob-bling on warped legs, or have lost a wing. One or two have a temporary artificial leg, to help them adjust. But they're perky and aggressive. A brown pelican named Pat – a lifetime guest who lost an eye and broke a wing when it was snagged by an angler's hook – is playing catch with a laughing girl volunteer, tossing a tennis ball back and forth. If anything, the bird is the better catcher, because its gaping maw looks like a jai-alai player's hand-scoop.

"Pelican Pat's been around so long she thinks she's one of the staff," the volunteer points out. "We had a gull that lost its wings, and Pat took care of it. Whenever the gull lurched over and fell, Pat pried it up with her bill so it could get back on its feet."

Pat loves to be picked up and have her head stroked; but her ladylike gentleness disappears when seagulls come swooping down into the pelican compound at feeding time. She puts the run to the gate-crashers by charging at them with her cavernous mouth wide open, like an infuriated steam-shovel.

How did Pat get her name? It just happened that when she was brought in so badly maimed, movie actor Pat O'Brien and his wife Eloise were visiting the site. They became the very first "corporate members" of the sanctuary organization.

At this moment a visitor emerges from the office doorway of a small wooden building nearby, so I say: "Well, guess it's time to drop in and see Ralph Heath."

"What?" exclaims a raucous voice behind me. "What? . . . What? . . . WHAT?"

It's Corky, another fish-crow, protesting as if he can't believe his ears. Why would anyone want to see an ordinary human when there are so many interesting birds to see?

The office, a former porch, is old, narrow and plainly furnished. At the far end sits the secretary, one of just four modestly paid staff workers. It's hard to believe that Ralph Heath, now entering his thirties, has operated this sanctuary since its founding in 1971. He still looks like a youth in his early twenties. Slight, with brooding dark eyes, tousled black hair and a full mustache that sometimes looks slightly droopy and sometimes a little bristly at the ends like a British Guards officer, he could be a younger brother of Burt Reynolds. Dressed as unpretentiously as his office, he's wearing a white T-shirt, khaki pants, slip-on shoes, no socks.

This dedicated humanitarian puts twenty-four hours a day into the job, seven days a week, all the year around, with never a vacation. But if you expected to meet an intense crusader for a cause, visibly aflame with inner zeal, you would be taken aback. Heath's manner is quiet, his conversation low-key; he doesn't get emotionally involved with every ailing seabird, because he'd soon be frazzled out – 42 per cent of them don't survive. There's plenty of time later to become fond of them.

Actually, many of his guests aren't seabirds – nor even birds of a different feather. A long list of former patients that were released at the rustic Brooksville refuge – headed by 303 Muscovy ducks and 188 mourning doves – ends like this:

Water turtles	4
Chickens	4
Snapping turtles	3
Gopher turtles	2
Bantam chicken	1
Water snake	1
King snake	1
Corn snake	1
Bull frog	1
Alligator	1

How on earth did an alligator crawl into the statistics? Ralph Heath explains, "A lady living on a lake south of St. Petersburg called us to say an alligator was stalking her dog. So we caught it, and looked after it until it could be freed in the inland preserve. Good thing she phoned us, too. It was six feet long and weighed 200 pounds."

A volunteer's head pops in the doorway.

"Want to see the cormorant when it comes?"

"Yes," replied Heath, "but better check our antibiotics now."

The head ducks out again.

How did he happen to start the sanctuary?

"Mere chance. One day my wife Linda and I were driving along Gulf Boulevard when we saw a cormorant limping along the side of the highway dragging a smashed wing."

"Hit by a car?"

"Possibly. Or it may have flown into a power line or a guy wire or even a window; a third of our bird injuries are broken wings. We took the cormorant to a vet, cared for him at home and named him Maynard."

Maynard became something of a celebrity. Soon people began knocking on the Heaths' door with disabled birds in shoe boxes, and the sanctuary was spontaneously launched. By the time Maynard died of a heart attack four years later, the haven had looked after 7,000 birds and was getting an average of fifteen patients a day from all over Florida – one for every daytime hour.

But devotion to his self-appointed task has cost Ralph Heath dearly. It's gobbled up his personal savings. It's forced him to sell most of the antique cars he collected as a youth. Above all, it's caused him to follow his chosen path alone.

"I don't blame Linda," he says. "I had her doing a lot – far too much. Not everyone wants to work at something every day, day in and day out. That's how the divorce came about."

Why do so many birds get sick or injured?

Occasionally they become ill from drinking water contaminated by sewage or industrial waste. Some, like cormorants which hunt under water, may be mutilated by sharks. Or like Centennial, one of the young bald eagles in the sanctuary, they may be attacked by another bird of their own species when they wander into its territory.

But mostly it's because of man. As Heath explains, "They crash into things they can't see; they get strangled in the plastic containers from beer six-packs; they get caught by fishing line – there are millions of feet of monofilament fishing line tangled up in the mangroves – or they get snagged by fishing lures they mistake for fish. We've removed as many as twenty fish hooks on one line from a pelican's legs and body. Sometimes a double-ended lure hooks both feet like handcuffs."

But these are crimes of indifference, neglect or ignorance. There are also the sickening ones – hard even to imagine:

Pampered kids who grab a young feeding duck and rip off a wing or poke a pencil through its eye.

A youth who tries to pick off tame park geese with a bow and arrow while his mother sits approvingly and eggs him on, and his father shoots a .22 rifle at bald eagles gliding through the sky – despite the fact that they are the number-one U.S. endangered species and are protected by state and federal law.

Guffawing boys who overrun fleeing pelicans with their outboard motorboats.

Men who toss giant fire-crackers (wrapped in bread) to flying gulls and laughingly watch their heads split.

Ghouls who wrap elastic bands around a captured gull's beak or bind its feet.

"Or," adds Ralph Heath, "the monster who throws handfuls of food to pelicans. And the next time throws a handful of broken glass.

"Once a choking pelican was brought to us. A witness said two men held it while a third shoved a beer can down its throat. I pulled the beer can out."

It's enough to make you lose your faith in human nature.

But don't.

Because Ralph Heath, who's closest to the picture, feels confident that these loutish freaks, including the men in the big cities and the backwoods who still run dog fights and pit gamecocks against each other to the death, are a dwindling species.

The great majority of people – a swelling, immeasurable tide of public opinion – has been rallying to the aid of dumb creatures. For evidence, just look at the gladly given help Ralph Heath receives. Look at the clean-cut representatives of today's younger generation, eight boys and girls who daily, without thought of pay, lug buckets of food and water to the birds and clean out the compounds. Professional veterinarians – twelve altogether – contribute their work in the operating room and lab converted from a garage. The sanctuary's lawyer donates his services too.

Seafood dealers save damaged crates of frozen fish for the birds. Shrimpers donate unwanted fish. Weather-worn, tough-talking crewmen of fishing boats, who in their old clothes, dripping water and silvery scales, look as if their hearts may be as hard as their appearance, keep a sympathetic eye open for convalescent ex-patients and go out of their way to bring maimed birds to the sanctuary.

So do rough-and-ready dock workers and truckers, policemen, firemen, school teachers, university zoologists, ecologists, marine biologists, federal and state park officers, the Coast Guard, Scouts, motel operators and maiden ladies – altogether as varied a group as you could imagine.

Other good friends give club luncheon talks to "spell" Ralph Heath, who can't accept all the invitations. A private airport owner provides a light plane and pilot so he can scour the coast for any injured birds missed during his patrols in the sanctuary's powerboat – including oil-spill victims that can be saved 80 per cent of the time if treated within twenty-four hours.

A member of the sanctuary's board, Pete Van Allen, drops in every week to collect birds that should be released in inland surroundings. He has freed thousands on his own 1,000-acre expanse of woods and lakes.

Another volunteer skilled in falconry teaches recuperating predatory birds, like hawks and owls, how to hunt rodents for themselves before being sent out on their own.

Even the palm-leaf roofing of the compounds is done free by a thatching firm.

With interested allies like these, it's little wonder that Ralph Heath feels a gradual change is taking place in the public's attitude toward wild life.

"And there's hope," he says, "this change will be accelerated by education and peer pressure – especially among the young."

"Peer pressure?"

"When members of a group look down on something, the other members won't do it."

Again the young volunteer's head bobs in, this time accompanied by an arm holding a giant metal pail brimful of flat shimmering fish slightly bigger than silver dollars.

"Can the pelicans eat these?"

"Don't see why not."

Head, arm and pail vanish.

How much does it cost to keep the seabird sanctuary going?

Surprisingly perhaps, seeing that some of the food is contributed, the grocery bill exceeds $1,500 a month, or $18,000 a year. This is because the birds devour 250 pounds of fish a day, along with dog food, vegetables, nuts, seeds, fruits, and patent energy food. But surprisingly, too, the entire annual budget of the non-profit Suncoast Seabird Sanctuary is kept down to $40,000, including staff salaries, utilities, and medicines.

To meet this bill, Ralph Heath and his directors pull out

all the stops. They seek public grants; they solicit contributions from individuals, service clubs, fraternal societies, Scout troops, church auxiliaries and the like; they have a U.S. tax-deductible "associate membership" plan of four levels from $10 (student membership) to $100 or more (sponsor); they have a card-carrying "Friends of the Birds" program for small givers; they've even adopted a popular charity device by launching an Adopt A Bird campaign to pledge people to pay for an individual bird's monthly diet – choose your own species.

This incidentally gives a clue to why the food bill seems high. It costs $7 a month to keep a great blue heron (one pound of sardines daily); $7 also for a brown pelican (one pound of mullet and herring); but if you want to be the foster parent of a royal tern, a smaller bird the size of a sea-gull, the price is still $7, because it must have a daily half-pound of special smelt.

The royal tern is often mistaken for a common gull. But it has a bright orange bill and a tufted black hair-do that stands up in the back as if it needed a little dab of Bryl-creem.

The most budget-priced boarder is an omnivorous seagull, at $4 (dog food and left-overs and donations).

"Oil companies have given generously," says Heath, "up to $5,000 in a single donation. And we're encouraged by the increase in public contributing. One old lady in New York sent a cheque for 67 cents."

How did he know she was an old lady?

"By the squiggly, tired writing. Oh, we get unusual gifts. Somebody – probably a youngster who'd seen a lot of cartoon comedies – sent us a miniature sailor hat for one of the pelicans."

But up to this writing, no really breath-taking gift has ever dropped down out of the sky, no gift big enough to make Ralph Heath's dream come true of a spacious new home for the sanctuary, preferably twenty or more acres in a secluded inland area, with the present site retained as a pick-up depot.

It's surprising such a bonanza hasn't materialized. For not only is Ralph Heath's sanctuary the biggest of its kind in Florida, but also it has pioneered in several important bird treatment techniques in such spheres as recuperative diets, alleviating shock, bone splinting, use of antibiotics, anaesthesia.

Experience has shown, for instance, that it's imperative to administer antibiotics immediately to seabirds mangled by fish hooks and to handle them very carefully in the early stages of recovery.

When Heath captures a badly wounded bird – often swimming after it from his power boat, long-handled net in hand – he snips and extricates the hooks, injects antibiotics and puts the victim on a soup regime, because solid food would kill him. This is no ordinary soup. It consists of ground-up fish, antibiotics, energy food, vitamins.

Oil-immersed birds are cleaned up with special chemicals and ensconced in a unique shallow tank designed by Heath, with soothing water coursing over its plastic seabed. In an emergency, the tank can accommodate 100 birds.

After a patient dies, veterinarians often conduct autopsies, and the results sometimes point the way to more effective treatment next time here or somewhere around the world.

The inevitable head pokes in again.

"Cormorant's here. Want to have a look? Breathing's heavy – pretty laboured."

As I follow Ralph Heath out, I remember to look around again for Doris the Duck. But the only duck in sight is a mother mallard in a fenced run, with half a dozen fluffy ducklings darting about and climbing back into her protective wing.

There are, however, all kinds of feathered characters. A bluejay, which has apparently spent too much time with woodpeckers in the lab, keeps desperately tapping on the post of his cage in the hope of coaxing insects out of the woodwork. Most birds seem to have personal names like Egie the Egret, Honky the Cormorant, Salty the Pelican – who runs up and gently nips you if you're paying too much attention to other pelicans and not to him – and, of course, Centurion the imperious, fixing you with an unwavering blazing glare until finally you turn your eyes away.

A year before – I remember well – we drove into Bay Pines Park one day to see the much-talked-about bald eagles' nest high up atop a huge gnarled tree. The massive cone-shaped nest looked very big from afar, probably four feet deep, but nature observers there told us it was really fifteen feet deep.

Then one day we read in a St. Petersburg paper about the tragedy. One of the baby eagles, strangling on a fish-bone caught in its throat, fell out of the nest (or was pushed out by its parents, so it wouldn't die there), and in the headlong tumble down to earth it smashed a wing.

Wildlife officers were quickly on the scene, hoping to save the stricken eagle even if it might never be able to fly.

We went back to Canada then, not knowing how the story turned out. It was therefore a genuine surprise the next winter to meet the star-crossed bird in the Suncoast Sanctuary, no longer a forlorn infant but now a handsome and majestic bald eagle.

Centurion cannot expect to drift through the clouds – but, as Ralph Heath points out, a bald eagle flies only to search for food, and Centurion has a lifetime supply assured. And some day, presumably, he will have a mate.

(Another little eagle fell out of the same nest afterward, stirring great anxiety among conservationists. However, it was a natural fall-out preparatory to using its wings. After regaining its breath on the ground and flapping around for some time, the eaglet revved up its engines and successfully took off into the wild yonder.)

Ironically, several attendants tell me about the bird the sanctuary is proudest of – but it isn't there any more.

This is Pax, a pelican and a very unusual one, for he was born in the sanctuary. His parents, Salty and Alexis, are officially patients Nos. 60 and 100, both disabled and grounded. To the delight of the staff, one day they performed their millennium-old mating-dance ritual: the female duly picked up the suitor's proffered sticks in her bill, sealing the bargain; and a big nest was duly built and two big eggs appeared.

Only a couple of days before hatching time, the soft-shelled eggs broke, evidently because of chemical poisoning in the parents.

Never discouraged, Heath launched the two adult birds on a special vitamin diet. And the next year a real live baby pelican pecked its way out of a shell.

The staff refrained from pampering or influencing the infant. They left the bringing-up job entirely to the parents.

And one day, at the age of three and a half months, the nine-pound brown pelican – wearing red tag No. 278 – winged upward from the compound, perched momentarily on a fence post, then atop a tall palm tree, circled the sanctuary three times as if to get a last look, then lifted away into the Gulf of Mexico's sudden sunset.

"The beauty of it," comments Heath, "is that the parents did it all."

But I realize the sanctuary will soon be welcoming a lot more newcomers, for in one pelican compound after another, a real Florida real estate boom is in full swing. Skyscraper nests are rising from the ground. The birds have even adopted the Florida condominium idea. In one pen two huge nests share a common wall. In each three-foot-high nest a pelican (male or female, nobody knows for sure) sits on the top leaves, cradling one or two or three eggs, completely oblivious of those goggle-eyed human spectators gawking through the wire fence less than five feet away.

Focus of public attention is a wriggling purplish transparent-looking bald blob – a baby pelican – loudly squalling for attention from underneath its parent's sheltering feathers. And is it well protected! Whenever another adult pelican walks by within a foot of the nest, the parent's long neck and long bill stretch out suddenly to astonishing length – like one of those old wooden lattice-work toys that reach halfway across the room when you squeeze the handle – and the intruder gets sharply nipped by nature's fish shears.

Yet among the sanctuary staff you sense an atmosphere of gloom. It's because a second baby pelican from the same nest was found outside on the ground this morning, dead – possibly rejected by the mother because it wasn't eating properly.

How do such elaborate nests get built in a bare compound? Easy. The attendants, hoping the feathered homemakers will take the hint, carry in baskets of sticks and twigs and leaves, and walk out. The expectant pelicans amble over and meticulously pick out the different sizes they want – big sticks for the foundation, lighter sticks for the upper storey, leaves for the top. When the construction projects are completed, they squat on them.

Today, at least, there's certainly no worry over whether the pelicans will get the hint. Courting seems to be the current fad. Love is bursting out all over. Here and there, almost everywhere, invalid pelicans are jousting and fencing in rivalry over mates and playing tug-of-war with nesting twigs. As many individual bouts are going on as in a National Hockey League rink-wide melee. Human observers can't tell offhand which are males and which are females, but fortunately the pelicans seem to know.

One bird even brings over a branch in its bill to offer it to a Chicago friend of ours looking in through the wire fence. (His wife says later, "I didn't know whether to leave Frank here for four weeks or waltz him out fast.")

Then comes startling news from a volunteer. A great blue

heron is nesting on two eggs – the first time anybody has heard of one planning to raise a family in captivity.

Not far away we hear a girl's low-modulated voice around the corner talking pleasant nothings with somebody – a boy friend, we know immediately, because human nature is the same the world over. When we peek around and look into a cage like a small walk-in shed, we see blonde Dianna King, down on her blue-denim knees, conversing softly with a red-tailed hawk, whose pen she has been cleaning. The hawk, looking as big close up as an eagle, and perched on a wooden rung, is staring back ferociously into her eyes from only a foot away. But, amazingly, every time she speaks he answers her earnestly in a throaty chirruping sound.

Dianna obligingly poses for a picture with an injured barn owl on her leather-gauntleted wrist, an owl with a face like a monkey, balancing itself upright by flapping the only wing it possesses while she talks to it reassuringly.

But now Ralph Heath is walking back toward his office, and I call out, "I'll follow you right in."

"Why?" shrills an indignant voice behind me. "Why? *Why?* WHY? WHY?"

It's irrepressible Corky the fish-crow. He catches me so completely off-guard I almost turn around and say, "Because we didn't finish our conversation."

I'm glad I did return, a few moments later, for I discovered an ironic thing. Ralph Heath, who's rehabilitated so many thousands of birds, who's regarded in the seabird world as an authority on their treatment and care, and who's been showered with humanitarian awards, can't treat them himself. He's a graduate zoologist of the University of Southern Florida, with training also in ecology, anatomy, ornithology. But he's not a veterinarian, so he can work only under the direction of a vet.

His father, Dr. Ralph T. Heath, Sr., a retired M.D., and his mother live in an upper apartment of Ralph Heath's duplex house. A colourful figure in pith helmet, plaid shirt and shorts, Dr. Heath circulates amiably among the visitors, looking like a Zululand park ranger on safari against the background of thatched huts as he hands out pamphlets and answers questions. Says the son affectionately with a rare smile, "He's our tour guide."

You get the impression Ralph Heath learned a lot from his father early in life. But the father comments: "*I* learned a lot from the birds. All of us could. They're kind to their young, they see they're warm and sheltered and fed, they keep them disciplined, yet they never raise their voices, and they never push them around."

My resumed interview with Ralph Heath is punctuated by phone calls as frequent as a taxi driver's gravel-throated radio messages. A woman in Seminole is worried about a strayed parrot high in a tree behind her house. . . . "We'll be there shortly." *Ring-ring-ring:* A man wants to contribute his party's catch of fish. . . . "Thank you, we appreciate it very much." *Ring-ring-ring:* A man in Largo . . . "Great; we're very glad you called." I say to Ralph Heath, "Does he want to give you fish too?" "No, he's bringing a load of old newspapers for the bottom of the cages." *Ring-ring-ring:* Busch Gardens would like twenty pelicans for its vast open compounds. *Ring-ring-ring:* Louisiana, the "Pelican State," has only a hundred eastern brown pelicans left. Can Ralph Heath spare some from the 250 in his backyard for the Baton Rouge Zoo? Immediately he arranges to ship twenty-five by air for a start. As they're disabled, they can't fly away from the zoo; but they can breed, which is pretty important for an endangered species.

I discover something common to every good worthwhile cause. Many people opposed the sanctuary vociferously. Local opinion was split. Some regarded Heath as a tourist asset; others damned him and his noisy birds as a nuisance. After a nearby motel complained, the small city of Redington Shores asked him to move.

108

Meanwhile the neighbouring small city of Indian Shores was saying, "Move here. We'll welcome you with open arms."

If Ralph Heath possessed a fairy godmother with a magic wand, the quandary couldn't have been solved more instantaneously.

He found that only one-third of his sanctuary was actually located in Redington Shores anyway. The other two-thirds was already across the civic boundary in Indian Shores.

So Ralph Heath simply moved a few cages of cormorants, herons and pelicans fifty feet over – and the bird migration to Indian Shores was completed.

It's time for me to leave. I bid my host goodbye outside his door.

"Bye-bye," repeats a hoarse voice from a fish-crow cage. "Bye-bye, *bye-bye*, BYE-BYE!"

But I can't resist pausing to watch the feeding of the pelicans – an unforgettable, eager, rackety spectacle. The attendant is toting in that huge metal bucket of flat fish, and he invites me in with him. All the pelicans swarm around, pressing on us like pet dogs at feeding time, clacking their bills in an incessant din that sounds like one of those Polynesian dances where natives bang bamboo poles together on the ground and the dancers nimbly jump in and out.

The attendant, whose name is Eddie, tosses the silver fish one by one into the wide-open waiting bills. I wonder at first which may get six and which may get none, but apparently he can tell by seeing the fish in each bird's jowly pouch for a few moments before it is swallowed. Besides, a satisfied bird will drop back to the rear.

It's amazing how awkward these pelicans appear on the ground. They look almost prehistoric, or as if they were designed by the creator of the square-built German Gotha bomber in the First World War. But in the air, as they coast low over treetops in precise single-line formation, they're

109

visions of grace that make beach promenaders stare up in admiration.

Now a strange one comes veering down into the compound and makes a perfect one-point landing – because it has only one leg.

"That's Pelican Pete," says Eddie offhandedly flicking a fish into Pelican Pete's waiting bill. "He was brought to us with fishing line wrapped around one leg, stopping the circulation. The leg had to be amputated. Now he often comes back at feeding time."

Suddenly Eddie thrusts the pail into my hands, hurries over to yet another pelican that has just alighted in the compound.

I see him working busily for several minutes, leaning over the pelican; then he comes back, and the big bird takes off again in a swirl of wings.

"It's peculiar," he says as I prepare to leave. "That pelican's legs were all trussed up in monofilament fishing line. It couldn't have survived very long."

"Well, goodbye," I say, "and thank you."

"BYE-BYE! BYE-BYE! BYE-BYE!" – the coarse voice from a fish-crow cage, anxious not to be left out.

"That's Eddie," says the attendant, smiling, adding matter-of-factly, "they named him after me."

"Just one thing," I interpose on a sudden thought. "That pelican with the snarled-up legs – did it just happen to drop in, or did it know enough to come to the sanctuary for help?"

"We don't know," he replies with a shrug. "We wish we knew."

The Mother
Instinct

A big bass broke the surface of Washademoak Lake and snapped at a little duckling, then at another. Both escaped death by split-seconds.

Just as quickly, the mother duck acted. She shepherded all her five youngsters up on her back and raced for shore. Clambering over the sand, she dumped them off, then kept flapping the baby ducks up the beach with her wings.

Everyone has heard how a mother partridge (ruffed grouse), confronted by a predator nearing her nest, will run away from it dragging a wing – as if it is broken and she can't fly – to divert the intruder into stalking her.

When you witness scenes like these, you can't help but feel admiration for the devotion, bravery and ingenuity of mothers of the wild.

In fact, modern scientists with all their endless resources have been unable to determine how an animal or bird mother imposes absolute discipline on her brood in the face of peril – any more than they can tell you how a cat or dog will sometimes find its way home from 200 miles away.

I sometimes think of the day I visited a mobile home in a North End trailer park in Saint John when we were shopping for a German shepherd pup.

"Well, you came to the right spot!" said the owner cheerily as we drove up. "The mother and her five pups are in the livingroom; I'll take you in, but really she's quite friendly."

We walked up the steps into the narrow mobile home, and went from the kitchen into the livingroom.

Not a dog to be seen.

It was eerie.

There were only three pieces of furniture in the whole room – a sofa and two upholstered chairs – hardly enough space for six dogs to hide behind.

But from both ends of the sofa I noticed the tips of black noses sticking out.

The owner bellowed, "Lady! Come out here! And all your pups!"

Suddenly the room was full of sheepishly penitent dogs, led by an amiable mother German shepherd that jumped up and put her paws on my chest and licked my face, as if to say, "Whatever you are going to do, be good to my family." She had heard the voices of strangers approaching and had communicated the "Danger – hide!" warning to her very young litter, who obeyed instantly.

As it happened, we didn't take one of those pups. But afterward I often found myself wondering how she did it.

The same thought occurred to me, years later, about Smokey the mother raccoon.

She ruled her four baby raccoons with such firmness that not one ever wandered out from under the garage into our German shepherd's run, only a few feet away.

It's easy to imagine, from talking with people who've raised tame raccoon families, what a demanding task Smokey had.

She had to bring up her children from mewling infancy, even as a human mother does, watching them discovering their hand-like paws and wonderingly feeling her face, quieting them when they complained they didn't get enough food or attention.

There came a night when she took them out into the open air to play like frisky kittens; to see how she washed her food in a water dish before eating it (some observers say this isn't necessarily because raccoons are so meticulously clean, or want to get the grit off but because they lack enough saliva);

and to follow her in line, like trunk-to-tail circus elephants, in their first brief foray into the woods.

Only one young raccoon, a mischievous imp we called Scamp, ever dared to be tardy.

Scamp loved to run up and down the mother's back before she knew what was happening, and to pull down the other baby raccoons when they climbed up to the top step of the dog's pen.

Sometimes the mother would give the signal for everyone to follow her, and three would obey immediately but Scamp would hang back, still scrounging around the lawn for food scraps, his nose going this way and that as if he was a rudderless ship. Then the mother would park the other three, motionless, in the tall grass bordering the woods and gallop down and send Scamp scampering up to join them, although I couldn't tell how she persuaded, prodded or punished him.

Owning a pet is great fun, an endless source of amusement, education and wonder. It is also an invitation to tears. Pets never live long enough, unless you have an elephant or a turtle. And if they are wild creatures that come out of the woods to your door, you are unable to protect them against their natural enemies or man's depredations. You can only look on helplessly as they grow up, sharing little fragments of their joys and sorrows, hoping no serious misadventure will overtake them; and secretly hoping – even if unconsciously – that they'll soon go away and relieve you of your worries.

I'm thinking particularly of one summer morning.

I should have known something was wrong.

When I took our dog Fritz out the back door at eight o'clock for his walk down the driveway, there was the mother raccoon looking out the opening under the garage – watching and waiting, still up and alert, even though it was broad daylight.

Obviously she was tired – she must have been keeping this

113

vigil for hours – because she was lying down and her head was propped up on a flat rock.

We continued on our way. As we reached the main high-way, a young hitch-hiker standing on the other side motioned with a nod toward a grey-brown curled-up shape lying silent in the middle of the pavement.

It was one of the young raccoons, dead – hit by a car that perhaps never even saw it.

When we returned to the house, Smokey was still under the garage looking out, like a statue. I phoned the local sanitation truck; and I tossed some dog treats to her, but she didn't pick them up. She was looking past me.

After another hour, at about 9.30, even though daylight made her more vulnerable to dogs and humans, Smokey emerged and hurried across the back lawn and into the woods to search.

I felt sorry for the young raccoon, but sorrier for the devoted mother, trying so hard to find the missing one whose body by now was on its way to the town dump.

My wife came out to the back door and said philosophi-cally, "Well, if *something* didn't kill them, the countryside would be overrun. That's the law of nature."

This didn't help my feelings much.

Nor, if Smokey could have understood, would it have helped hers.

That evening at dusk the mother raccoon had her brood out busily feeding on the lawn again.

"You see," my wife said, "just like a cat who's had a kitten taken away, she'll get over it quickly."

After a moment's reflection she added, "But I don't think you will."

And she was right. Because the whole family was there – all but little Scamp.

How to
Beat a Bigger
Opponent

A man is lucky in an emergency to have a wife like mine. She has the courage of a tigress. One rainy evening in the 1930's, as a nurse-in-training at Montreal, she was confronted near the old Royal Victoria Hospital by a heavy-set hold-up man. He grabbed at her purse. "Your money or I'll blow your head off!" The nerve of the fellow made her so mad she chased him all the way down the hill, whacking and jabbing at him with her umbrella.

So when a loathsome wild creature invaded our summer cottage at Epworth Park on the St. John River, I didn't lose my cool. I kept calm. I knew any crisis would be handled okay.

It was a harrowing experience, nevertheless, hearing it coming in the darkness.

The hour was just past midnight.

Our long bedroom occupied the second floor under the

eaves, with a window at each end of the room. My bed was close to an unfinished wall where the chimney went up, and my head was almost against the wall boards.

The first sign I noticed was an eerie, scraping, slithering sound by my head, as if something sinister was trying to squeeze between the shingles and boards and get into the room.

The quiet noise went on and on. The Thing, whatever it was, possessed awesome determination.

I thought of a snake . . . or a weasel . . . or a strange bird . . . and then it dawned on me: A bat!

At that very moment I heard a soft *plop* on the floor beside my bed.

I jumped out into the middle of the room, yanking the light chain on.

It *was* a bat. Instantly it began flitting up and down the room from end to end, past me and then past my wife, and back again.

"Mildred – a *bat!*" I yelled.

I plunged back into bed, pulling the covers over my head.

I waited confidently.

In the far distance I heard a muffled voice: *"You* do something. The bat will get in my hair!"

It was a disillusioning turn of events. Apparently wild crocodiles or rampaging rhinoceroses are one thing, but with a bat, a husband is on his own. As every woman knows, it's far more important to save a new hair-do than save your husband.

Of course I knew that any resourceful husband could easily deal with a bat. After all, it's only a mouse with wings.

I had a wonderful inspiration.

Grabbing my top blanket, I leaped out of bed and held it up in front of me like a net to trap the bat.

The bat flew right over my shoulder.

My pajama pants fell down. I bent over and pulled them

up – there was no time to fasten the drawstrings – then wheeled around to face the bat and held up the blanket again.

The bat zoomed past my ear.

Down went my pajama pants. I retrieved them, righted myself, turned around with the blanket upraised.

Past flew the bat at what seemed to be supersonic speed. My pajama pants were around my ankles again. Wearily I pulled them up.

All this time my wife was to be seen only as a misshapen mass bunched somewhere under several blankets. Every once in a while a faint voice said, "Did you get the bat?"

On and on went the exhausting game . . . until eventually I realized, to my chagrin, I was losing. I was panting and, after each pajama pull-up, gulping for air. The bat had more stamina than I did.

Just as I was about to collapse, the bat disappeared down the winding narrow stairway.

I staggered down and grabbed a broom, and looked for it to deliver the coup de grâce.

Finally I espied the culprit. There it was, hanging upside down from a wooden rafter in the livingroom!

I got a dustpan to catch it when I hit it. But suddenly the bat dropped down into the dustpan without a blow being struck. It was fagged out.

Carefully I carried it outside and deposited it on top of the rubbish heap with all the ceremony and respect due a valiant foe.

Then I slowly climbed back up the stairs and slumped into bed, completely done in.

My wife, reappearing at long last, asked where the bat was. After I told her, she went downstairs and outside with a flash-light. She reported the bat had already flown away.

But I couldn't get up. I was still gasping. I couldn't fly away.

Which only shows how a four-ounce bat can beat a 220-pound man.

It should be worthy of the *Guinness Book of Records*.

After all these years, I just thought to ask my wife how much money she saved by risking her life and refusing to hand over her purse to the Montreal hold-up man.

"Oh, I don't know – less than a dollar," she said. "That was in the Depression, and any student nurse who had a dollar was rich."

That Dangerous Wild Creature, Robin Redbreast

The nest under the eaves of our cottage verandah at Epworth Park was built before I even noticed it.

Sitting in the nest, on the top beam at the end of the verandah, was the mother robin. I didn't have the heart to shoo her away and demolish the straw-and-mud home after all that work; besides, she probably had eggs under her. So we let her stay, eight feet up from the floor – silent, immobile, implacable – eyeing everyone with an unblinking stare that went right through them.

Wasn't I lucky? An instant brood of pets to befriend – right on my own front porch! I could hardly wait for the little birds to be born so I could take out treats to them.

We were so considerate of the expectant mother that we even asked all our friends to come around to the back door. Some grumbled; but they could see how happy the feathered family was going to make me.

One day, peeking from a distance while the mother was away, I saw tiny heads and beaks poking above the rim of the nest. They had arrived!

121

I was thinking about them that night before I dropped off to sleep in our upstairs bedroom. Then–

CRASH!

The cottage shook.

CRASH! CRASH! CRASH!

All I could imagine was that there was a belligerent drunk at the front door – or that Halifax, Nova Scotia, was having more explosions in its naval munitions bunkers. Years before, during the Second Great War, accidental blasts there had reverberated across the Bay of Fundy to Saint John with such impact that, as the news of the day noted, a 250-pound grandmother was shaken out of her bed.

CRASH! CRASH!

I ran down the stairs, flashlight on, and out the front door-way.

An unbelievable sight met my eyes.

Huddled low on the nest was the mother robin, her wings spread protectively out on each side, gazing straight down.

Staring back at her, only a foot and a half below, was the McWilliams' cat, desperately clinging to a crossbeam by the claws of one paw while pummelling at the nest with the other paw.

"Get!" I roared.

The cat dropped down to the floor, and streaked away into the darkness.

Impulsively I hurled the flashlight after her, and it landed in the bushes. Fortunately, as the flashlight was turned on, it was easy to locate in the raspberry patch. (I don't urge bird lovers to follow my example and retrieve a flashlight at night from the bramble bushes, especially if they have bare legs and bare feet.)

My immediate problem, of course, was how to protect the little family against further attacks.

An inspiration hit me.

There were two crossbeams between the nest beam and the

floor. To get up to the second-highest beam, the cat had to leap up to the lowest and then to the second.

I hurried out back to the garbage barrel, dug out all the old tin cans, and filled them with water from the rain barrel. Then I arranged them in rows all along the two lower beams, like an ingenious tank trap. If the cat tried to jump up again, it would upset the cans, and water would shower down – and everyone knows how cats cringe from water. Besides, the clattering would wake me up.

As I didn't have quite enough old cans, I went out to the kitchen pantry and opened a fresh can of minestrone soup, a can of beans and a can of spaghetti, and poured the contents into glass jars and put them in the wooden ice-box.

While I was stacking the cans – my water bombs – on the two beams, the mother robin kept looking down at me rigidly, never moving, her wings still extended.

Then I thought of the beach umbrella at the opposite end of the verandah! Seven feet tall with a huge spread, it was just the thing to lean against the wall directly under the nest. No animal could possibly climb up through it to get at the birds.

Happily, I set it against the wall, while the mother bird's black eyes regarded me piercingly from only inches away.

And then in a mad pounding swirl of wings the bird flew at me, jabbing my head, nose and neck with its beak, whacking my head and shoulders mercilessly with its wings for trying to get at the nest. It was everywhere at once. I was stunned, I couldn't believe it. How could a robin do this to its only benefactor, its friend in need?

Helplessly I yanked my pajama coat up over my head and staggered backwards toward the screen door of the living-room.

From one wooden pillar to another I gyrated, blindly feeling my way toward the door while taking blows to the ears, the solar plexus and the kidneys. Bizarre anxieties raced through my mind: What would the neighbours think? The awful thought occurred to me that with my head veiled, midriff bare, pants loosely tied below the belt line as I whirled along the verandah in apparent abandon, they might assume I was practising Turkish belly-dancing at 1 A.M.

I groped to the screen door, flung it open and fell in. At that moment the great umbrella, wheeling along after me in the slip-stream, stopped in front of the door with the handle pointing directly at the screen.

On the top of the handle only inches away through the screen, appeared the mother robin, glaring at me as if daring me to come out and start making trouble again.

"You can look after your own damn family!" I said loudly.

"What did you say?" My wife's concerned voice from the head of the stairs. "Who are you talking to?"

"I was talking to a robin."

"Oh."

She just looked at me as I stormed up the stairs and went to bed.

A person who befriends a family of nature's creatures has to undergo a great deal of misunderstanding. It's part of the penalty of being kind; it's an ordeal that tests a man's mettle.

For instance, those open jars of soup, beans and spaghetti in the ice-box – I explained to my wife in great detail next morning the purpose behind them, but she still looked at me the way she did the night before, with the same strange expression, shaking her head slowly, her arms hanging limp.

And those thirty cans of water on the verandah crossbeams – I assured her we could put them in the garbage in about six weeks, as soon as the baby robins flew away. She didn't make any comment, though I was sure I heard her say to herself as she went by, "This too shall pass away."

The neighbours were even less perceptive and understanding. Anyone with half an eye could see the cans were put

124

there to prevent a cat from climbing up. But Sam Blackburn, walking idly by and noticing the cans lined up, stopped, did a double-take, surveyed each row, noting the diverse labels on the canned vegetables and fruits, and finally said: "Is it fun playing supermarket?"

Walter Bollard was no better. He paused and frowned and stared, walked up close to tilt his head back and get the labels in the focus of his lower bifocals – Catelli Spaghetti, Campbell's Chunky Minestrone, Heinz Beans. Finally he drew back, studied the two rows as a whole, and in a voice barbed with skepticism said: "Is *this* Modern Art?"

By chance I was glancing out the front window the day the fledgling robins, over-heavy for their sparse wings, fluttered down from the nest and hopped around the verandah floor.

I rushed out the back door with a bag of small stones to throw at the cat if she tried to intercept any of them while they were helpless on the ground.

Strolling along, I stayed well behind the mother robin as she hop-skipped beside her brood, in case she misinterpreted what the stones were for.

My wife was looking curiously out the diningroom window as we went by, and I said, "I'm staying with the baby robins while they learn to fly."

I can't be positive, again, but I'm almost certain she said, "Why don't you flap your arms?"

Thank goodness – after only a hundred yards of hopping, the youngsters seemed to get the knack, and flew weightily up into the low bushes like overloaded planes, and then higher into the shrubbery branches.

I walked back delighted and relieved, and found my wife rushing the cans into green plastic bags for the garbage man.

"I phoned him," she said. "He's making a special trip." Apparently the idea was to get them out fast before I could put them back again.

It was then I discovered, when I heard a plaintive *mew*, that the McWilliams' cat was following along behind me, her tail up straight except for a slight spiral on top, like smoke coming out of a chimney on a fine clear day. Evidently she had been prowling along after us, out of sight of both the robins and me. When the birds flew away, she had followed me home. When I stopped now, she rubbed her head against my knee and curled her tail around my legs.

At first I supposed (trying to make myself think in the ridiculous ways animals do) that she was sympathizing with me because she didn't get a good chance to get at the birds and I didn't get a good chance to get a shot in, either, with my stones.

Then it occurred to me, especially when she kept mewing: She thought I might be good enough to raise another robin family for her so she could have better luck next time.

That's what *she* thought.

You, Too,
Can Win Attention

Do you feel lost in the crowd? High-hatted by people who should speak to you? Ignored by everyone? Unable to make an impression?

Take a tip from Buster, a British Columbia raccoon who lives not far from us.

He can get attention in a split-second.

Buster's the pet of a family who moved across the continent to the Atlantic coast. Bigger and darker than New Brunswick raccoons, he lives like a sultan in the Arabian Nights. He has his own spacious home inside the modern garage, his own gleaming oval-shaped entrance doorway framed in white metal, and his own outdoor run. His daily gourmet meals are meticulously prepared – a hard-boiled egg, carrots, celery, a quarter-head of iceberg lettuce, and so on, even to three sweet-filled cookies for dessert.

Whenever his owners let him go free in their carefully man-icured courtyard, which includes a swimming pool, Buster ambles around and – with the contemptuous disdain of

Henry VIII throwing chicken bones over his shoulder – digs up plants right and left and turns over sections of lawn sod, obeying an instinctive urge to look for grubs.

They know if they admit him into the house, they'd better shut all the doors, because Buster enjoys nothing more than rummaging through closets as if looking for articles that might be put up at a garage sale.

I took some children to see him one day, and the first thing he did was to startle me by scurrying over, seizing my thigh in a raccoon version of a bear-hug squeeze, then as suddenly scurrying away.

"That means he likes you," the owner happily explained. "That's how he shows affection."

I wished he'd told me before.

Then, unexpectedly, one of the children found to her surprise she was no longer holding the plastic bag she'd brought full of marshmallows and other treats for Buster.

He'd whisked it away from her so fast she didn't know it.

Now he was walking past the pool, muttering imprecations to himself . . . *rumble-rumble-growl-grumble.*

"That means, 'I've got it now and no one better try to stop me,'" interpreted the proud owner.

I wondered aloud how they'd ever persuade such a formidable animal to go back into his run if he didn't want to go.

"Very simple," said the owner; and from his side pocket he plucked a bag of potato chips. He didn't even take out a chip. He just crackled the plastic bag – and Buster raced for the open gate leading into his run.

"He can't wait. He loves potato chips," the owner pointed out.

But if it's an idyllic life for Buster, the same can't altogether be said for the human family the sultan rules.

They stored a canoe on top of Buster's outdoor caged run; they rescued it a day later after he had somehow removed the ropes holding it on.

Buster's big discovery was what he found on the wall of the garage. It resembled a handle of some kind, so naturally, being a raccoon, he pulled it down to see what would happen. It was a switch. The adjoining residence was plunged into darkness. People came hurrying to find out what was the matter.

Buster never learned that the lights went out. All he learned was the important thing: that a yank on the switch would bring people running to see him. So now he has solved the problem of loneliness. He can have companionship, day or night, with the flick of a paw.

A family at Lepreau on the Bay of Fundy coast thought it was hilarious when their pet raccoon learned how to jump up on a verandah windowsill and ring the doorbell. They encouraged him by bringing tid-bits every time he rang – lobster legs, chicken bones, left-over halibut, bacon fat.

Now it *has* become hilarious.

They don't know what to do. It's either disconnect the doorbell or keep on being jolted out of a sound sleep at four o'clock in the morning by insistent rings, as if there's an emergency in a neighbour's home – only to find their pet happily waiting on the doorstep, accompanied by sons, nephews, cousins and assorted friends, all agog with anticipation.

The point is that raccoons are extremely perceptive, astute and dextrous.

In Fundy National Park on New Brunswick's rock-girt coast, it's well known among the rangers that raccoons go for the "new" campers.

The reason is that newly arrived families often don't know enough to keep their left-overs and garbage securely safeguarded from nature's scroungers.

At his home near Spruce Lake, Robert E. (Ted) Austin has watched a pet raccoon jump to a ledge in the porch three feet from the floor, reach over and shake the door handle back and forth, and finally pull the door open as the spring lets go – just to let the dog in.

"Then," says Mr. Austin, "it gave the dog a swipe with its paw, just for fun. It also took a friendly poke at the cat."

For play, his raccoons love to dodge under the couch in the livingroom, turn over on their backs and go sliding from one end to the other, using their four feet on the bottom of the couch to propel themselves.

"We've often had them in the house until they were six or seven months old. They were gentle, slept peacefully, very clean – they always went to their own box – and there was no smell.

"They'll go swimming with you; if you leave the house first, they'll track you by following the dog scent, which is stronger than human – you can't lose 'em.

"We've always handled the younger ones like a mother cat would her kittens – lift by the scruff of the neck and support them underneath, to prevent being nipped; you can put them up on your shoulder and they'll run around and sit on your head. They're nice and warm – warmer than we are."

People are often astounded, Ted Austin comments, by how raccoons manage to lift very heavy metal lids off garbage cans.

"I've seen them employ engineering principles to do it. A raccoon who can't raise the top off will slide up the pail backward, hook his hind-leg claws over the top, and get results by using the leverage, the weight of his body, and the angle as he pulls with his front claws."

Ted's son, Donald, who lives at Musquash, a few miles farther down the Bay of Fundy, adds: "My father parked a truck in back of our house one evening by the raccoon's home. When the raccoon found it couldn't reach the truck with its front paws, it simply backed itself up to the hood and disconnected the distributor cap off the engine with its rear legs. They're doublejointed in the rear legs, you know.

Also it pulled the wires out of the headlights, and put them in its 'dog box.' "

A pet raccoon is a lot like the Scarlet Pimpernel. Now you see him, now the elusive pet has vanished. The Austins once housed their raccoon in a former outdoor bathroom. "We left a crack in the roof rafter only three inches by fifteen inches wide for ventilation, and this full-grown raccoon of about thirty-five pounds squeezed through and came to meet my wife when she arrived with food for him in the evening."

One great drawback about befriending raccoons is they'll come back bringing their children – and their children will bring their children. That's what happened to Mr. and Mrs. Donald Patterson on Sandy Point Road, a rural section of the city of Saint John.

"We've had as many as twenty-five at one time," Mr. Patterson remarks.

"Why so many?"

"We feed 'em."

That was early this year. By the laws of mathematical progression, they may have fifty raccoons by now.

Have they had any regrets that they ever started acting as godparents to so many?

"Not exactly; but we feel bad about the number of raccoons we see with a leg missing. They've mostly been caught in traps, and gnawed themselves free. It's very sad, because a three-legged raccoon can't climb well, and has difficulty in digging. A raccoon needs four paws."

What has been the most rewarding memory?

"The absolute trust shown in us by raccoons in trouble. There was a baby raccoon that came out of the woods, its mouth as prickly as a pin cushion with dozens of porcupine quills. It probably couldn't eat at all. It would have starved to death.

"I put on heavy gloves and held the little raccoon at arm's length, while my wife first cut the quills – they're full of air, and you can't pull them till they're clipped – and then she extracted the barbs, one by one, with pliers.

"The job took three evenings, and the baby raccoon came back out of the woods to us every time.

"When my wife finished, we both remarked on the same thing: The little raccoon had never made a whimper. It seemed to know we were doing it a favour."

Wut-wut
Got There First

Everyone around Pocologan on New Brunswick's Bay of Fundy coast knows about Mrs. Clara Shaw's pet seagull Peter, alias *Wut-wut.*

How did he get two names? Well, Peter was his given name; but many people called him *Wut-wut* because that's what he said . . . *"Wut-wut, wut-wut."*

For several years before her death, Mrs. Shaw put out a daily dish of food on her back step for Peter. His customary perch was on top of the angled roof of the garage, where he waited to see what he was getting.

He posed there minute after minute, silent and perfectly motionless – so aristocratic-looking that a tourist from Vermont remarked: "That's a pretty nice piece of work."

"What is?" asked Otty Goodeill, Mrs. Shaw's brother-in-law.

"That weather vane. It's very life-like."

"It *is* alive." And to the visitor's surprise, Peter swooped down and alighted beside his dish.

Clara Shaw adamantly refused to chase Peter away, even though he messed up the garage so much she had to pay out hundreds of dollars for a new roof.

But the really memorable thing – what they still talk about – was that whenever Mrs. Shaw left in her car to visit her sister Mrs. Thompson in Dipper Harbour, nearly twenty miles away, Peter (or Wut-wut) always got there first; he was waiting for her. He seemed to know instinctively where she was going. It was easy to beat the car, naturally, because the highway is a winding route following the coastline and therefore much longer than as-the-gull-flies.

Mrs. Shaw's brother-in-law, a genial man with smiling eyes behind gold-rimmed spectacles, lives only a couple of hundred yards away in Pocologan. He worked forty-two years in the old Shaw and Ellis clam-packing plant before he retired.

"Oh, yes," he told me. "I've often heard that story. Peter now comes to *our* garage, you know." He pointed to the breadcrusts lying in the grass beside his back step.

Just then a large white and grey gull glided in and set itself down on the rooftop of his garage.

"Here we are!" Mr. Goodeill exclaimed, squinting through his glasses. "Peter, is that you?"

Peter, if it was he, gladly coasted down and selected a big crust and soared away with it.

"So hard to tell," ruminated Otty Goodeill, frowning through his glasses in the sun as he followed the gull's upward flight. "They look so much alike."

There's no doubt that seagulls, like most seabirds, are astutely observant. They have to be, to survive. They can angle-dive and pluck a scrap of food off a salt-water wave more efficiently than any mechanical pick-up that man has been able to devise. I've taken a mackerel off the hook while fishing near Campobello Island in Passamaquoddy Bay, and suddenly found to my surprise there was no fish in my hand – it had been "lifted" by a pirate gull as unobtrusively as by any of Fagin's young pickpockets. I was conscious only of a passing shadow.

And as for perceptiveness: If you walk down to a Florida beach carrying a small plastic bag of breadcrusts, gulls even at a far distance will watch you closely. If you make any move to dig into the bag they'll come flocking toward you and past you, then wheel around to keep their wings undulating slowly while they mark time, stationary, above your head. When you toss a dozen crusts up in the air, a dozen gulls will catch them before they fall to the sand.

They'd be great stars as big-league outfielders. I sometimes wonder which gulls are more adept at picking off treats in mid-air – the ordinary white-grey variety or the vehement black-hooded "laughing gulls," which look as if they're out to rob an armoured truck. Both will shrill and scream and bawl you out unmercifully if they get to know you and you offer them nothing.

Yet, on your way back to the cottage, the empty plastic bag now filled with interesting seashells, the gulls pay no attention to you.

Gulls, as I said, are seacoast pirates as well as useful scavengers, nature's own beach clean-up crew. They love to rob birds' nests of eggs. But so do men, sometimes out of necessity. A traditional pastime on Grand Manan island, at the entrance to the Bay of Fundy, was gulls'-egging – the methodical gathering of eggs from seagulls' nests in the cliffs. Many a grown-up businessman of today who hails from Grand Manan can remember having hearty breakfasts of three or four gulls' eggs at his boyhood home, and watching his mother use gulls' eggs to bake a white cake that had a deep orangey hue – as the gulls' eggs themselves did when the shrimp, one of their favourite foods, were running.

Every Grand Manan youngster a generation ago knew how to be sure his basket of gulls' eggs was fresh. A gull lays three eggs in succession; therefore, the gatherers took eggs only from nests that contained one or two.

Wild ducks and geese often become pets – especially if

they're fed regularly. Some people insist that these birds get "imprinted" – that they believe their benefactor is their mother, and accordingly follow him or her everywhere.

I think this happens only when the ducklings or goslings are very young – later they just know a good hand-out when they see it, and keep looking for it. They're not above using flattery – even on an automobile.

When Bennet O'Blenis drove home every suppertime to his house in Westmount, a suburb of Sydney, Nova Scotia, he always tossed treats to two wild mallards that swam around a brook pond.

Not unexpectedly, the ducks began to associate the arrival of the car with food.

Soon, whenever it was heard turning in, the ducks would come winging over the rooftop and alight in the yard. Then, ignoring the driver after he got out, they'd waddle around the car, quacking excitedly to it in *duk-duk-duk* talk, apparently confident that if they showed enough affection for the car, it would tell the man to feed them.

In the south, as in Canada, you see wild birds that have adopted the human race – not because they were imprinted but because it's the easiest way to catch food.

Many a Florida home has a daily back-door visit from a tall, spindly-legged white egret – a bird of infinite patience that walks with exaggerated frontward- and backward-leaning deliberation, like a slowed-down movie of an old-time police sergeant majestically patrolling his beat. It often pauses to listen and wait silently for several minutes, which leads passers-by to think that, like the Pocologan seagull, it's an ornament – this time a plaster or metal lawn knick-knack.

But of all the wild birds that have become boon pals of man at times, my favourite for some reason is the brown pelican.

If you notice a man casting out a line from a Florida shore, you may also notice as many as five or six pelicans, waiting, watchful and wise, hopefully paddling very slowly three or four feet away from him, regarding him fixedly side-on with one eye.

Driving beside the Intracoastal Waterway only an angler's cast from the Gulf of Mexico, you may see the backs of three sitting fishermen huddled together on the bank, waiting for a strike. But look more closely. The bigger one in the middle is the father; the smaller one on the right, his son; and the small one on the left, a pelican.

The man and boy are delighted; they think the bird is fascinated by their skill at fishing. As a reward, they throw him any fish they don't want to keep; he swallows it in several laborious gulps, and his human friends watch with interest to see the lump travelling down his neck.

The pelican, for his part, is delighted to humour them. He knows they won't want to keep all of the fish they catch, anyway. And it's a lot easier to sit and watch and flatter people than to work for his dinner.

You Can't Be
Unlucky Forever

I got stung on my foot by a bee this week – and, boy, did I ever feel good!

You see, one of the heaviest strains on our home life has been the fact that insects always prefer my wife to me. She couldn't understand this, except there seemed to be something unfair about it, especially as she reacted severely to all kinds of bites and stings.

She didn't blame the insects. By some strange intuitive process of reasoning known only to women, she blamed me.

In travelling, when we went into a motel where a family had a dog the night before, we always woke up in the morning in the same plight. My wife had seven flea bites; I was unscathed.

"Why don't they bite you?" she asked me accusingly.

I couldn't answer. I could only hang my head in shame. Heaven knows, I'd done my best; I slept on top of the covers with only my pajama top on, surely an inviting target, but as always I was ignored; I didn't get bitten.

My wife claimed also I wasn't of much help to her in avoiding insects; but I'm sure this was only irrational thinking, the result of being harassed so often. Deep down she knew I always tried to be her staunch protector.

For instance, one summer day I was bringing our black German shepherd, Karl, through the kitchen back doorway of the house. Just as I opened the door, holding him on the leash, a yellow-jacket wasp spiralled up lazily from his fur.

In an instant I grasped the situation in my mind: Swat the wasp and prevent it from bothering my wife!

Swiftly grabbing up a rolled magazine that had served as a gentle "spanking stick" when our dog was a pup, I swung it with unerring power and smacked the wasp, sending it in a line drive right across the kitchen – into my wife's mouth.

It stung her before she knew what happened.

Next day when her face had swollen, I pointed out happily, to cheer her up, that at least she could always count on me to do everything possible to protect her; but I seemed to tell from her expression she wasn't cheered up much. As it happened, she wasn't speaking to me.

There appeared to be no end to my unluckiness.

Later, when we were driving ten miles from home with my wife at the wheel, she suddenly grasped one of her pant legs.

"A bee!" she yelled as the car swerved. "I've been stung!"

I tried to be helpful. I said, "Don't put us in the ditch."

She kept grabbing her leg as the car braked. "I've been stung again – and now again!"

When the car came to a halt, there was the bee walking around the floor mat by our feet.

"Kill it! Kill it!" my wife said to me, still holding her leg.

Anxious to do the thing properly, I got out of the car, opened the back door and rummaged around the back seat, looking for the rolled-up magazine. I couldn't find it. When I returned to the front seat to tell her, the bee was gone.

"It probably flew out of the car," I said.

"No, it's around – it's still here!" my wife insisted.

You can see how easily wives become distraught; they won't listen to calm common-sense.

As I climbed out of the car on arriving home, I saw to my

surprise a bee was crawling around the floor mat.

"There it is!" my wife shouted. "Kill it!"

"But I don't think it's the same one," I remonstrated. "It may be another bee."

My wife stepped on it – bang! But for reasons she didn't explain, she seemed to hold a grudge against me.

Things at home didn't improve noticeably after I wrote a book called *Ghosts, Pirates and Treasure Trove*. No sooner did the book appear than inexplicable happenings started to befall me. The trouble was that many of the strange occurrences involved my wife, too. Our car radiator burst when we were driving through Moncton, eighty miles from home. A big slab of plywood flew off the top of an approaching truck and wafted through the air directly toward our windshield, then up-ended at the last moment and only sideswiped the car on my wife's side.

A TV commentator in Moncton jokingly suggested that maybe I had offended one of the ghosts in my book. Other interviewers took up the refrain, and eagerly predicted more calamities.

Only a day later I was in the back porch when a terrific explosion erupted behind me in the kitchen. Slivers of flying glass struck my back.

I wheeled around to discover my wife standing dazed by the stove, her hair full of glass fragments, her long housecoat glittering with glass – and a dead partridge bouncing off her head and her shoulder and down to the floor.

Winging at top speed, the bird had crashed through the big dual-glass windows with such projectile force it swept dishes off the kitchen sink and littered the downstairs with glass that took three hours to clean up.

Of course we didn't attach any significance at all to such minor accidental goings-on; but it was sort of a relief just the same not long afterward to head for the south and start a new season afresh in new surroundings.

It almost seemed, however, as if our jinxes had travelled in the back seat south with us.

In a motel room, fleas materialized again in the night – and again it was my wife they preferred.

In despair, almost pleadingly, I asked an exterminator who drove in the next day, "Why don't they bite *me*?"

He shrugged as he kept spraying the carpet from his portable hose outfit. "Nobody knows why; all the guys in our business just know that fleas would rather bite dames."

We arrived in the south – but no sooner had we started taking daily walks in our swim suits on the ocean beach when my wife stepped on a bee.

It was no fun for either of us. I was in disgrace again.

By now I had almost lost hope for my redemption.

Once I stood up to my knees in the calm gulf seas when eight rays or skates of some kind, bat-like black fish with long rat tails and gently undulating wings – two or three feet wide from wing-tip to wing-tip – swam in as gracefully as a corps of ballet dancers, looked at my shins, and just as effortlessly swam away. I guessed they weren't the stinging kind. I'd been snubbed again.

But every lane of bad luck sooner or later has to have its turning.

The very next day, as we sauntered along the beach, I felt a sudden burning in the sole of my foot.

"Good lord!" I cried happily. "I've been stung!"

"Don't be ridiculous," my wife said. "You never get stung."

"Look" – I hopefully held up my foot.

A two-second silence.

"You *have* been stung," my wife exclaimed in wonder. "Scrape your foot on the sand in case the stinger's still in it! Walk in the surf. The salt water will help! I've got marvellous antibiotic ointment at the apartment. We'll go right back!"

My life was suddenly transformed. I could hold my head

up again. I was out of the dog-house, or in this case the bug-house. I marvelled at the stroke of pure luck that had got me stung. Was it an absent-minded bee? Or was it fooled by my new musk after-shave cologne?

"There it is!" my wife cried as we turned to walk back. "There's the bee crawling right in front of you. Kill it!" And she hurried away.

In a moment, hobbling appropriately, I caught up with her. "Wow, my sole feels as if there was a red-hot needle in it!"

"*Now* you know what I went through," my wife said with satisfaction. "I'll look at it when we get back. Walk in the surf! Did you kill the bee?"

"I sure did."

Really, I didn't. How could anyone kill an insect that did him such a favour?

Hitch Up
the Moose, James

John Connell, a colourful New Brunswick hunting guide, and his friend Daniel Lloyd were trekking on snowshoes through the Bartibog woods near the Newcastle-Chatham highway one day in March 1910, when they came upon a one-year-old cow moose floundering in deep snow.

They hauled out the weakened animal, which might have soon died of starvation. Connell led it home to his barn to recuperate on a diet of tender bush shoots and warm bran mash for the rest of the winter – and for some unexplained reason he named her Tommy.

Tommy was domesticated quickly, and became fond of the whole Connell family. They trained her to pull a sled, and even travelled to Chatham in their moose sleigh one afternoon.

A year and a half later Tommy disappeared into the woods, and the skeptics had a field day. They chorused, "We told you so all along – you can't tame a wild critter that big."

Two weeks afterward, Connell was out guiding some American "sports," as they're called in the Miramichi country, when he heard a crashing in the woods. On a hunch he called out, *"Tommy!"* – and she plunged through the underbrush to come right over and then follow him.

Not long afterward Connell thought of using Tommy as a decoy on hunting trips. It was a mistake. Immediately she attracted a bull moose – but an excited neighbour, out hunting alone, fired at the bull and accidentally killed Tommy.

John Connell wasn't the only man in the Maritime Provinces to train a moose. In Fredericton old-timers say that one of New Brunswick's early lieutenant-governors, Sir Arthur Hamilton Gordon (1861-1866), was certainly the only official representative of Her Majesty the Queen who ever drove through a provincial capital in a sleigh hauled by a moose.

At Irishtown in the Moncton area in the early part of this century lived Philip Sellick, a latter-day Paul Bunyan who could stare down a bear and bend wild animals to his will; he was often featured at harness meets in demonstrations of how fast his moose, driven by him in a homemade sulky, could travel around race-tracks.

His great-nephew, author Lester B. Sellick of Halifax, recalls also that Amherst, across the Nova Scotia border, was the home of the celebrated John (Moose) Kent. "He tamed moose and trained them to haul sleighs and carriages but was never quite able to subdue their suspicious irritable nature."

That's putting it mildly. The last moose he trained galloped away across the Tantramar Marshes, leaving in its wake a trail of splintered wood and twisted hardware as the sleigh completely disintegrated.

John F. Gough of Fairview had no better luck with his pet moose but he did manage later to recover his damaged sleigh as well as the unhurt moose.

Lester Sellick can recount the exploits of several other Nova Scotia moose-tamers, including a Yarmouth man who frequently raced his moose at harness meets in direct competition with horses.

The real point of all this, to me, is not that the big wild critters can be tamed – or almost. It's that man will try to befriend and train anything that walks, flies or swims. And he'll usually insist that, although few people realize it, his pet really is the most intelligent you ever saw.

I've met people who swore to this with complete seriousness

about iguanas, eagles, cobras, gorillas, cougars, sea lions and frogs. I've enthusiastically patted husky dogs on a cross-Canada hiker's double leash – until he told me they were wolves, and explained he hadn't mentioned it before so I could see for myself how gentle and smart they were.

In fact, the best way to start a heated argument guaranteed to ruin a perfectly good party – apart from well-worn topics like politics and religion, abortion and marijuana – is to say you read somewhere the dolphin is the cleverest animal in the whole world. Promptly you'll be batted down by a man who assures you killer whales are so intelligent you don't even have to use the reward system in training them; and as for gentleness they're entirely misnamed, as "killer" is merely a corruption of an aboriginal name. Proponents of every species will claw their way into the controversy, which will go on until someone announces he has it on indisputable authority that the pig is the smartest. This usually ends it, because so few guests can answer from the experience of having had a pig as a pet.

Like most of my friends, I grew up in an era when sensible people believed implicitly no animal could be smarter than the family dog. I marvelled at the braininess of my first pet, Togo, a sizable short-haired fawn mongrel. Once he was standing in the middle of the tracks when a streetcar came up behind him and bumped him in the rear. Ever after that, whenever he heard a streetcar coming around the corner, he quickly backed up across the sidewalk against the shingles of our house as if to say, "Now let's see if you can get behind me and do that again." You have to admit no streetcar ever managed it.

I should have thought again about dogs' cleverness after I visited Andrew (Beef) Malcolm's house. Beef was Canada's outstanding shot-putter. He hadn't arrived home when I dropped in. His mother, proudly showing what the dog knew, said, "Where's Andrew?"

147

The dog immediately trotted all around the rooms, looked in the open closets, carefully searched the fireplace – and then, to my astonishment, stood up on his hind legs and looked in the top of the floor-stand ashtray. (Beef, I might have mentioned, is a big man, then weighing well over 200 pounds.)

Smartness, of course, isn't everything. I love dogs anyway, and although I tell myself every time we get a new one, "This is going to be our last," I know that some day my very last one will survive me.

But every so often I feel I've had enough of pet-raising. I've been through so many ordeals – like the one every dog owner knows, of walking the dog outdoors on the leash endlessly up and down, up and down, waiting for him to heed nature's call so everyone can get to bed . . . and you know what happens: I put so much mental effort and concentration into urging him on, I suddenly feel I have to run, and I race home, hauling the dog, and rush headlong past my wife, who's asking, puzzled, "Did he go?"

And puppyhood! Those continual newspapers laid on the floor . . . I brought home from the newspaper office so many old copies from all over North America that my neighbours expressed amazement at how well read I must be by now and consulted me respectfully on the significance of world events.

When I took the pup out in the March snow, he ravenously gulped down snow.

I called the vet. He said, "If he eats too much, he'll get sick."

That's what I thought. That's why I called him.

Came spring and the snow melted. I took the pup out on the gravel – and he gulped down gravel.

I called the vet. He said, "If he eats too much, he'll get sick."

Now, I believe that veterinary surgeons, considering their

skill and the heart-rending tasks they're called upon to do, deserve every cent they earn. But the resulting bills reflect the strange scale of values we ascribe to today – or at least, the figures appear to.

My wife was in hospital for a serious operation that kept her there for two weeks. When she came home, taking into account our Medicare and Blue Cross, her total bill was $17.

Our cat came back from her operation the same day; her bill was $35.

It shows who's important in our modern society.

But back to my dogs: Perhaps not all of them were especially distinguished for intelligence.

I remember Jock, my wire-haired terrier who followed the embarkation parade of the Fighting 26th Battalion through the streets of Saint John to their ship in the First Great War – and apparently embarked with them, as he never came back from the parade.

And there was Sport, a neutered spaniel we all wept over when she leaned glaze-eyed against a post of the cottage verandah, obviously near death's door from a mysterious malady. The only slim clue was bits of coloured tinsel dangling from her jowls. We rushed her to the vet, who told us she was drunk. Later we learned she had lapped up several glasses of beer on a neighbour's verandah floor, and for good measure wolfed down a pound of boxed chocolates.

Shane, our red silky-haired Irish setter, had fantastic tracking ability. Let out of the house into the snow an hour after someone had left on a through-the-ice fishing hike across the frozen expanse of the Kennebecasis River, he'd catch up in no time two miles away. Shane was also a great retriever; the trouble was every day he kept retrieving other people's plastic bags of garbage, depositing them all neatly by our back porch so we could pay the garbage man by the size of the load.

Shane's proudest moment was on a New Year's Day when

he traipsed home, head held high, carrying in his mouth a lady's corset. We never found out whether somebody threw it in her garbage or whether by mischance she lost it during the New Year's Eve celebration. We duly paid the garbage man to take it, and tried not to look at him.

When we brought Shane up to my father-in-law's farm at Salisbury, the first thing the dog did was race out and confront twenty Guernsey cows in the pasture. Just like musk-oxen confronted by a predator, the light brown cows formed a solid straight line facing the dog. Then, as automatically as if a football quarterback had given the signal, they lowered their heads – and horns – waiting for the charge. Fortunately my father-in-law ran out and snatched away the setter. But I've always thought of the confrontation since as an outstanding example of intelligence – on the part of Guernsey cows.

Karl, our first German shepherd, I'll always remember because he looked into your eyes so intently trying to figure out exactly what you wanted him to do. One day when our two cats unearthed a nest of baby chipmunks, I shouted at them as they ran past me and each of them dropped a chipmunk. We were able to round up most of the young ones and put them in a pail. Then, in order to go after the others, I called Karl.

"Here, look!" I said. "Mind the chipmunks, Karl. *Nice* chipmunks. Don't let them get out" – and I gently pushed back one that was crawling over the side top.

Karl got the idea immediately. For the next half hour he stood guard over the pail, never taking his eyes off his charges, and frequently bopping one back with his nose when it threatened to climb over the side.

One drawback about Karl, it turned out, was that the plumber, Mr. Wanstead, had the same first name, though we didn't know it at the time.

Once when we called the plumber he got out of his truck and started in the back door – just as our dog tried to squeeze in too, past his legs.

"You get *out* of here, Karl!" my wife exclaimed loudly, her finger pointing accusingly. "You sneak, don't you try any of your tricks on *me!* Beat it!"

The plumber drew back in astonishment, and kept backing up toward his truck.

Botsy was a German shepherd owned by my wife's family in Salisbury, New Brunswick, when she was growing up, and Botsy had a special job. At that time Salisbury was heralded as "the Silver Fox Capital of the World" – huge specialized fox ranches stretched across the landscape, and many farmers also raised foxes as a sideline.

On the Stiles dairy farm Botsy was a watchdog, a cattle rounder-upper and a silver-fox retriever.

Once when a midnight intruder partly opened the back door, and reached his hand in to work on the chain, Botsy silently took hold of the man's wrist in his teeth – and held on. The would-be burglar's howls brought the family.

But Botsy in his conscientiousness overdid some things. He was unexcelled at running down escaped silver foxes that had dug under the guard-fence. At close quarters he always out-foxed them; he knew which way they'd dart. In a longer chase, a fox backtracks and cross-tracks and leaps so his pursuers can't follow his scent. Botsy would circle and wait till his quarry came back, then down him. While the fox desperately gnawed at the thick ruff of his neck, Botsy would signal – *"Bark! Bark! Bark!"* – for the farm hands to come and get the captive.

The only trouble was that Botsy in his zeal sometimes ran down wild red foxes too, which at that time had little value. And early one morning the family, hearing the familiar triumphant barking, hurried out of bed to find Botsy had cornered a rat in an outside summer kitchen. It kept jumping and jumping in a corner, and Botsy kept facing it, waiting for his owners to come and praise him for keeping the rat unmarked, alive and in such good condition.

Our two cats were smart, too – if it served their self-interest. One day the eleven-year-old mother – three-legged because of an amputation after being caught in a trap – and her nine-year-old daughter were chased around the house in a desperate race by two whippets.

Everyone knows how phenomenally fast whippets are.

But incredibly, these Persian cats were just as fast. The mother darted under the verandah – she could squeeze in farther than even a thin dog dared go. Her tortoise-shell daughter rounded the house a whisker ahead of the nearer whippet, then soared up six feet high over the wire fence into our German shepherd's run – and sat there beside her good bristling friend the police dog, while the whippets looked on from a safe two feet away on their side of the fence.

Another time – speaking of resourcefulness – the three-legged cat was trapped by a strange golden retriever out in the grassy field. There was a swirling blurry flurry of fur and feet, and the cat streaked for home with the dog snapping at its tail. But the cat didn't head for the closed screen door of the kitchen porch – she knew she couldn't open it. Instead, she headed straight for our dog dozing on the lawn – and as she reached him she did a sharp-angled right turn. Her pursuer piled up on top of her sleeping protector – and the explosive result can be imagined.

Many a cat or dog owner has taught the family pet to get up and ring the doorbell to be let in, a happening that never fails to surprise and delight guests. But one New Brunswick household got a surprise itself when the doorbell kept ringing after supper, and the lady of the house told her visitors, "Oh, that's only the cat." At that moment the family cat came out of a bedroom and put a paw on her knee, looking her straight in the eye.

She went to the door, and came back to say with a sigh: "It's the neighbour's cat that our cat pals around with. It learned from our cat how to do it. Our cat was asking me to let it out because its friend was calling."

Some people will avow their pet crow is the smartest creature ever – but it always seems to come down to a built-in miser complex.

My wife's family had a typical instinctive collector. Blackie, brought up from infancy, lived in the woodshed all winter, fed with the chickens, refused to come in the house. But he followed the children when they tended the garden. If they picked peas and beans, he'd be right with them, snapping off pods for himself and flying away to a safe vantage point to eat them. But the hoarder's hankering for bright things was always dominant; he'd fly through any open bedroom window and snatch jewellery, especially Grandmother Colpitts' thimbles. Repeatedly the family found newly washed laundry lying in the mud: somebody had swiped all the clothespins off the line. It was like hitting the jackpot one day when they found the swollen secret cache under the gnarled roots of a big old tree where Blackie had stashed everything away for his old age.

You get an idea how many people are wild-life devotees when you talk with David Christie, natural science curator at the New Brunswick Museum in Saint John. He was able to direct me offhand to people who had befriended almost any native species you could name – the Burzynski family in Moncton had a tame ovenbird; Arthur Callaghan of Musquash had a pet ruffed grouse, or partridge, that came when called; and as a matter of fact, Mr. Christie himself at that moment had a young barn swallow, preening and chattering and sitting on his finger at his desk (its nest had been torn down in a West Saint John garage before it was able to fly; he was feeding it hard-boiled eggs mixed with yarrow from the garden).

Countless people are devoted to the horse, even if few will claim it leads the world in intelligence. Certainly some have good reason to be grateful to old Dobbin. Like my wife, who recalls, "On a blizzardy winter day when we were going to a country school near Moncton, someone would bring the horse and sleigh from the farm to take us back – and he'd just 'give the horse its head' in the storm. The horse would always get there and turn in to the right driveway."

The horse, of course, is a deeply-ingrained creature of habit. I always remember a mustachioed young swain of the early 1900's whom our family knew well. He was ostensibly a very religious man. When he was invited to our home he was always the one who offered to say grace, even though we couldn't make out a word of what he was saying. He sounded like air bubbles rising to the surface – or like Bing Crosby singing "Boop, boop, *boop, boop, boop.*" But it was deeply impressive, and we felt the better to start eating.

He was courting a girl who lived in the suburbs. Sometimes when she was busy he would borrow her parents' horse and gig and go for a little jaunt himself in the Golden Grove district.

The next Sunday when the young man called for his

betrothed, and they took a romantic spin together into Golden Grove, the horse dutifully turned up into the driveway of Saint John's most notorious house of ill-repute and patiently halted at the hitching-post.

Though I'm fond of raccoons, I've never become familiar enough with these pets to put my hand in their mouths and feel their teeth or to let them lick the peanut butter off my fingers as my younger daughter-in-law does – or let them lick honey off my cheek.

But I've fed enough pelicans by hand to know these tame birds mean you no harm – unless you happen to be getting too close to their young, as I unwittingly did at the Suncoast Seabird Sanctuary while taking snapshots of the setting great blue heron in the next compound. Every time I bent over, I jumped as I felt a sharp pinch in the rear – a father pelican's neck and beak had stretched four feet.

Pelicans are amazing creatures. In three and a half weeks a baby pelican can grow startlingly – from a little shapeless purple blob that emerged from a shell the size of a goose egg, into a lusty five-and-a-half-pound white bird clad in snowy down, big enough almost to crowd its parent out of the huge nest, and mature enough to squawk angrily at passing pelicans and jab at those that seem too close. In less than a month!

I enjoy watching pelicans cruising nearby while I'm fishing. They miss nothing. Whenever anyone pulls up a shimmering silver fish, they all open their huge bills wide by automatic reflex, just as a dog drools.

Nobody, to my knowledge, has ever tamed an eastern panther in New Brunswick – or has anyone photographed one. For most of a century, between the mid-1800's and early 1900's, they were believed extinct in this province . . . but evidently a dozen or so survivors had lurked in the timberland recesses.

Scores of people in recent years have reported seeing them,

footprints have been plaster-casted and definitely identified by the Smithsonian Institution in Washington.

The nearest I came to seeing one was one morning seventeen miles deep in the woods on the Sevogle, a branch of the Miramichi River. To our surprise, a truck pulled in to our remote salmon-angling camp. It was the forest ranger. He was excited: "Boy, do you know what I just saw? An eastern panther, crossing the dirt road right in front of your cabin! I stopped my truck and grabbed my rifle, then I realized I wasn't allowed to shoot. It was a huge cat with the longest tail-drag I ever saw!"

I was alarmed. Our elder son and his wife were due anytime from Nova Scotia with their two-year-old son. If we were away fishing and they innocently let the youngster play outside the camp . . .

The ranger saw my concern and hastened to allay it. "Of course, if it was a panther I saw," he assured me, "it would be twenty miles from here by now, they travel so fast. But do you know what I think? I really saw two wildcats, walking one behind the other – that's what I saw! They just *looked* like a panther."

Two wildcats weren't too much comfort, either.

After leaving a warning note, we fished that day in complete security as far as we personally were concerned, because after all we were up to our hip-rubber boots in rushing waters (and you know how cats like water). Besides, we were in a valley between sheer thirty-foot cliffs.

Not until the next week did I discover from naturalists: (1) eastern panthers love swimming; (2) they can easily leap thirty feet in one pounce.

At least, we told ourselves that day as we fished, the panther was twenty miles away by now.

Then, unexpectedly again, a Jeep drew up to our camp door that afternoon, its driver a mining engineer. He blew in robustly.

"You fellas know what just crossed your road? Lord – the biggest damn cat I ever saw, and dragging a long tail!"

As I said, many people have seen eastern panthers – including our younger son and his wife beside the Trans-Canada Highway one June day just out of Amherst, Nova Scotia, on the Truro side. It was cat-like, a deep rusty brown, the size of a big German shepherd, dragging a long tail and walking unhurriedly along the edge of the woods as numerous cars whizzed by no more than fifteen feet away.

But back to pets: I was grateful to my brother Ian, who brought me revenge at long last on my mother's ladies' sewing circle. They met at our house once a month when I was a young boy, and it was my mother's delight to dress me up like Charlie Chaplin with a stuck-on felt black mustache and an oversize derby hat – a painful procedure to me – so I could send the ladies into hilarious gales of laughter by singing "Peggy O'Neill," with my hands on my heart and then with one hand reaching out to them.

My brother had a pet white mouse. He never even gave it a thought, because it had free run inside his shirt, and it was clean and harmless.

Just before I was to come out for my star turn, my brother appeared in the parlour in front of my mother and said, "Do you know where my skates are?"

At that moment the white mouse chose to emerge between his front shirt buttons and critically look over the assemblage of ladies, left and right:

Eek! Shriek! Scream!

Women jumped up on sofas and chairs. One landed on all fours on a coffee table.

When order was restored, the sewing circle went on sewing. No one, happily, ever thought of calling for Charlie Chaplin (or any of his brothers) again.

If a prize is ever awarded for the greatest patience in taming a wild creature, it surely should go to Mrs. Nancy

157

Mickelburgh of Beaver Lake Refuge in the upper Loch Lomond area, not far from Saint John Airport.

When Mrs. Mickelburgh saw two beavers building a dam years ago, she resolved to become their friend. She offered them poplar branches; they vanished. One morning she noticed they had cut down an apple tree, so she offered an apple at the end of a long pole.

Finally a beaver accepted the gift. So Mrs. Mickelburgh kept shortening the pole until, one day, a beaver was eating out of her hand.

It sounds easy, perhaps. But altogether it took four years.

Today Nancy and Ernest Mickelburgh live beside a long lake created by the beavers. Fifteen thousand visitors a year come for the free entertainment of watching Mr. Mickelburgh call the beavers at feeding time – "Come *up,* Eddie Shack! . . . Come *up,* Flip Wilson! . . . Come *up,* Queen Victoria!" And they swim up the lake with their kits, and waddle on their hind feet around the crowd on shore, taking the proffered treats of carrots and apples, each looking for all the world like two gigantic front teeth supported by a coarse-haired body.

One of the oddest master-and-pet relationships I've seen was when Anthony, the famed Buccoo Reef guide in Tobago, took us wading through waters filled with schools of tiny tropical fish. Nearing a cluster of rocks, the massive black man said, "Now I'll show you my special friend" – and he held out his hand under water toward a crevice. Out swam a sparklingly brilliant jewel fish to cavort around his fingers as if it knew him well – which Anthony claimed it did.

I acquired a wild fish pet myself, if unintentionally. We were salmon-angling on the Sevogle, but I couldn't get past a ledge where you had to walk around a cliff face; it was so narrow I'd have overbalanced into the rushing waters.

So while the family went on, I contented myself by dangling a fly in front of the nose of a salmon idly swimming against the current in a bathtub-sized rock formation smoothed by centuries of swift-moving water. He wasn't interested. He just kept eyeing me.

The idea occurred that I might very, very gradually get the long cone-shaped landing net around him from the tail up, if I moved as slowly and imperceptibly as the hands of a clock.

It took great patience – but half an hour later he was totally ensconced in the net, still keeping his tail slowly fanning.

The voice of the devil whispered in my ear: One mighty heave out now, and it would be mine – a twelve-pound Atlantic salmon! There was no game warden for miles around. We had our licences – I could always say I hooked it. Just one heave . . .

But I couldn't. I'd spent so much time with this salmon that now we were friends; I couldn't play such a mean trick on my own pet salmon.

I swished the net back off the big fish, and still he didn't panic. He just kept looking at me as if he knew me all along better than I did.

The salmon, however, wasn't my most unusual pet. In Florida I had a cricket in the bathroom that stopped chirping when I walked toward it; and a digital clock radio that stopped playing when I walked away from it. The radio was the bigger problem. It was exasperating. I tried to sneak away in the dark, but it always knew; it faded out almost completely. My wife suggested, seriously I think, that I take it to bed with me.

Once she woke up at 1 A.M. to find me piling heavy luggage and books on top of a footstool I'd moved over to the dresser in front of the radio.

"What on earth are you doing?"

I said, "I'm trying to make the radio think this is me because of the weight on the floor."

She said, "Lord," and fell back on her pillow.

On a subsequent night I awoke to find my wife standing by the dresser piling jewellery on top of the radio. I was alarmed: I thought she was making it an offering to try to coax it to behave.

"I'm trying to improvise an antenna," she said, adding her earrings to the heap. It didn't do any good. The radio refused to be bribed.

Later a radio repair store told me the human body acts as an antenna. It was deflating. I always thought the radio liked me.

I never solved the mystery of the elusive cricket. But I noticed that when the police helicopter clackety-clattered over at midnight, it always chirped back. It thought the whirlybird was a baritone cricket.

It's impossible to escape the conclusion that the so-called smartness of some wild life exists only in the onlooker's doting imagination.

I remember the tethered bear at a Salisbury service station that always held a dishpan over its head when it rained.

This sent lady spectators into ecstacies of admiration. One ran to her car and said to the menfolk: "Come quick and look – this is the most intelligent animal you ever saw!"

The men strolled over. "Just watch!" urged the lady. They formed a half-circle around the bear. Nothing happened. To encourage him to show his intelligence, the woman brought over a kitchen chair and put it beside him. "There's a nice chair," she said.

All eyes upon him, the bear put the chair over his head and looked through the rungs.

"What did I tell you!" cried the admiring woman. "He means he's a captive; he's in jail."

Then the bear picked up the chair. He broke all the rungs off it. He broke the seat in two. He deposited all the remains in a pile, then he sat on it.